Cinzia White

Dazzling

New York Beauty

SAMPLER

Paper Piece a Show-Stopping Quilt • 54 Blocks

C&T PUBLISHING

Text and artwork copyright © 2021 by Cinzia White
Photography copyright © 2021 by C&T Publishing, Inc.

Publisher: Amy Barrett-Daffin
Creative Director: Gailen Runge
Acquisitions Editor: Roxane Cerda
Managing Editor: Liz Aneloski
Editor: Kathryn Patterson
Technical Editor: Julie Waldman
Cover/Book Designer: April Mostek
Production Coordinator: Zinnia Heinzmann
Production Editor: Alice Mace Nakanishi
Illustrator: Cinzia White
Photo Assistants: Kaeley Hammond and Lauren Herberg
Photography by Estefany Gonzalez of C&T Publishing, Inc., unless otherwise noted

Published by C&T Publishing, Inc., P.O. Box 1456, Lafayette, CA 94549

Library of Congress Cataloging-in-Publication Data
Names: White, Cinzia, 1958- author.
Title: Dazzling New York beauty sampler :
paper piece a show-stopping quilt : 54 blocks / Cinzia White.
Description: Lafayette, CA : C&T Publishing, [2021]
Identifiers: LCCN 2020029469 | ISBN 9781617459788 (trade paperback) | ISBN 9781617459795 (ebook)
Subjects: LCSH: Patchwork--Patterns. | Quilting--Patterns. | New York beauty quilts.
Classification: LCC TT835 .W493 2021 | DDC 746.46/041--dc23
LC record available at https://lccn.loc.gov/2020029469

Printed in China
10 9 8 7 6 5 4 3 2 1

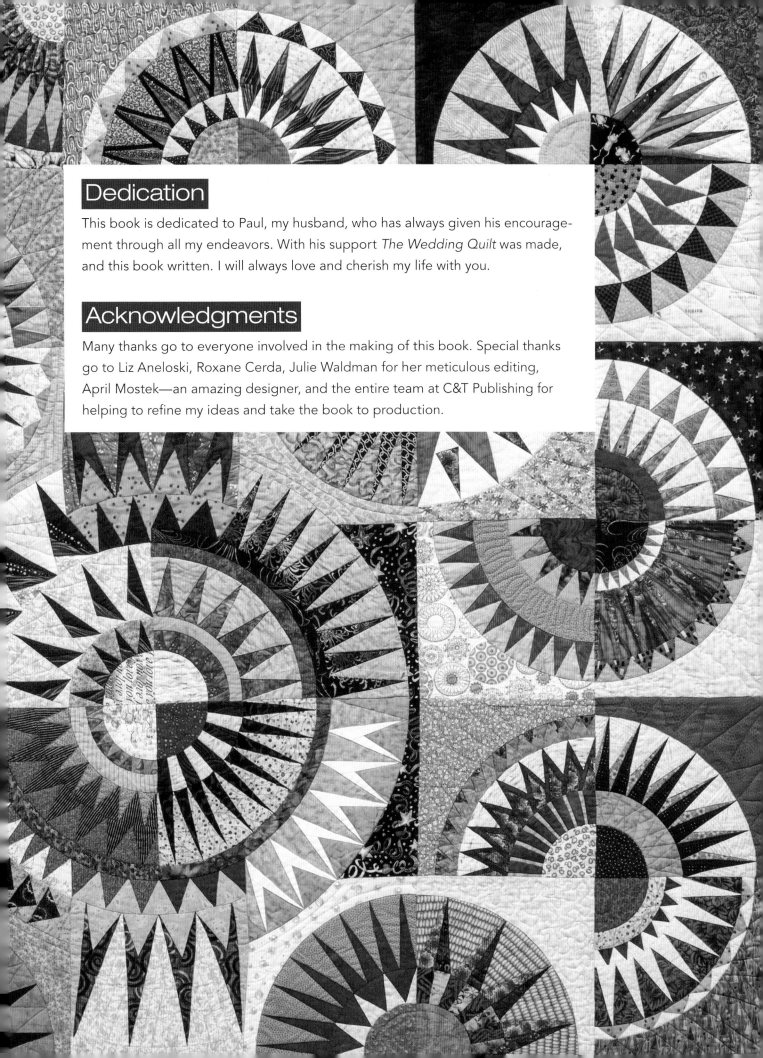

Dedication

This book is dedicated to Paul, my husband, who has always given his encouragement through all my endeavors. With his support *The Wedding Quilt* was made, and this book written. I will always love and cherish my life with you.

Acknowledgments

Many thanks go to everyone involved in the making of this book. Special thanks go to Liz Aneloski, Roxane Cerda, Julie Waldman for her meticulous editing, April Mostek—an amazing designer, and the entire team at C&T Publishing for helping to refine my ideas and take the book to production.

Contents

Bogan Moth (A1) **14**

Kangaroo (B1) **19**

Numbat (C1) **24**

Honeyeater (D1) **31**

Galah (E1) **34**

Bottlenose (F1) **39**

Jellyfish (G1) **44**

Crocodile (A2) **15**

Wombat (B2) **20**

Lizard (C2) **25**

Wedgetail (D2) **31**

Emu (E2) **35**

Bilby (F2) **40**

Cuttlefish (G2) **45**

Platypus (A3) **15**

Green Tree Frog (B3) **20**

Dugong (C3) **25**

Peacock (D3) **32**

Wallaby (E3) **35**

Frillneck (F3) **41**

Sea Dragon (G3) **45**

Redback (A4) **16**

Glider (B4) **21**

Bluebottle (C4) **26**

Magpie (E4) **36**

Bandicoot (F4) **41**

Pipistrelle (G4) **46**

Brolga (A5) **17**

Flying Fox (B5) **22**

Cassowary (C5) **27**

Black Swan (E5) **37**

Ghost Bat (F5) **42**

Emu Too (G5) **46**

Koala (A6) **17**

Hairy Nose (B6) **22**

Redback Too (C6) **28**

Peacock Too (D6) **33**

One Eye (E6) **38**

Fruit Bat (F6) **43**

Dingo (G6) **47**

Lyrebird (A7) **18**

Lizaroo (B7) **23**

Kingfisher (C7) **29**

Blue Whale (D7) **33**

Hairy Nose Too (E7) **38**

Koala Too (F7) **43**

Sheathtail Bat (G7) **47**

Pelican (A8) **18**

Fairy Penguin (B8) **24**

Possum (C8) **30**

Possum Too (D8) **34**

Tasmanian Tiger (E8) **39**

Echidna (F8) **44**

Glider Too (G8) **48**

General Information

Finished quilt: 96″ × 106″ • **Finished block: 10″**

The Wedding Quilt by Cinzia White

The Wedding Quilt

This quilt was made to celebrate the wedding of our son Paul-James to the delightful Khanam. Our other son, Richard, thought it should be called *The Anniversary Quilt* to acknowledge the fact that it wouldn't be (and wasn't) finished in time—a common occurrence when I become lost in the fun of a quilt.

● **Tip: Seam Allowances**

○ A ¼˝ seam allowance is used within each arc and when joining arcs.

○ A ½˝ seam allowance is used when cutting fabric for the pieced arcs and also on all edge pieces of the blocks. A seam allowance has been included in fabric quantities.

	A	B	C	D	E	F	G
1	Bogan Moth A1 (page 14)	Kangaroo B1 (page 19)	Numbat C1 (page 24)	Honeyeater D1 (page 31)	Galah E1 (page 34)	Bottlenose F1 (page 39)	Jellyfish G1 (page 44)
2	Crocodile A2 (page 15)	Wombat B2 (page 20)	Lizard C2 (page 25)	Wedgetail D2 (page 31)	Emu E2 (page 35)	Bilby F2 (page 40)	Cuttlefish G2 (page 45)
3	Platypus A3 (page 15)	Green Tree Frog B3 (page 20)	Dugong C3 (page 25)	Peacock D3 (page 32)	Wallaby E3 (page 35)	Frillneck F3 (page 41)	Sea Dragon G3 (page 45)
4	Redback A4 (page 16)	Glider B4 (page 21)	Bluebottle C4 (page 26)		Magpie E4 (page 36)	Bandicoot F4 (page 41)	Pipistrelle G4 (page 46)
5	Brolga A5 (page 17)	Flying Fox B5 (page 22)	Cassowary C5 (page 27)		Black Swan E5 (page 37)	Ghost Bat F5 (page 42)	Emu Too G5 (page 46)
6	Koala A6 (page 17)	Hairy Nose B6 (page 22)	Redback Too C6 (page 28)	Peacock Too D6 (page 33)	One Eye E6 (page 38)	Fruit Bat F6 (page 43)	Dingo G6 (page 47)
7	Lyrebird A7 (page 18)	Lizaroo B7 (page 23)	Kingfisher C7 (page 29)	Blue Whale D7 (page 33)	Hairy Nose Too E7 (page 38)	Koala Too F7 (page 43)	Sheathtail Bat G7 (page 47)
8	Pelican A8 (page 18)	Fairy Penguin B8 (page 24)	Possum C8 (page 30)	Possum Too D8 (page 34)	Tasmanian Tiger E8 (page 39)	Echidna F8 (page 44)	Glider Too G8 (page 48)

Block layout

About Fabrics

New York Beauty is a traditional block that will work with any combination of colors and prints, as may be seen from *The Wedding Quilt*. The important thing is to have a distinct difference between the points and the surrounding section.

Choose 100% cotton as it handles well and is easy to finger-press.

To minimize color run, prewash and press the fabric.

Requirements are based on 40˝-wide fabric. The required seam allowance used throughout is included in the cutting measurements.

A large variety of fabric was used in *The Wedding Quilt*, which makes it difficult to provide exact quantities, as many may be cut from scraps and from one piece of fabric.

Fabric for the individual blocks is presented with instructions for each block. *All fabric quantities include enough fabric for one extra wedge of each fabric in every pieced arc.*

FABRIC FOR THE BLOCKS

Fabric quantities are approximate only.

- 15 fat quarters of assorted blue prints and batiks

- 15 fat quarters of assorted green prints and batiks

- 10 fat quarters of assorted red/orange/pink prints and batiks

- 6 fat quarters of assorted yellow/orange prints and batiks

- 6 fat quarters of assorted white/cream/beige/yellow prints and batiks

- 5 fat quarters of assorted black prints with colored elements

- 5 fat quarters of assorted aqua/teal prints and batiks

- 3 fat quarters of assorted purple prints and batiks

- 1 fat quarter each of yellow/orange stripe and black/gray stripe

Supplies and Tools

- Foundation paper (such as Carol Doak's Foundation Paper by C&T Publishing) or lightweight woven Vilene

- Clear adhesive tape (such as Scotch Removable Magic Tape) for joining foundation papers together

- Freezer paper (such as Quilter's Freezer Paper Sheets by C&T Publishing)

- Fabric starch or starch alternative (such as Heaven Scent Spray Starch by Eppiflex Australia or Mary Ellen's Best Press)

- Rotary cutting tools

- Add-A-Quarter ruler (by CM Designs)

- Several new sewing machine needles

- Bookmark or piece of heavy cardboard

- Tweezers for removing paper

- Mechanical pencil

- Fine-tip permanent markers (such as Pigma) for fabric

- Fabric scissors

- Craft scissors

- Resealable plastic bags

- Iron and ironing board

- Basic sewing supplies

● Tip: Thread Color

○ *When joining light fabric to light fabric, use a light-colored thread.*

○ *Similarly with dark fabric to dark fabric, use a dark thread.*

○ *However, when one seam joins both light to light and dark to dark, use a light-colored thread. Afterward, use a matching pen to color the thread, if it is showing, between the dark sections.*

● Tip: Working with Directional Prints

When a directional fabric, particularly a stripe, is used in two neighboring units, it is often preferable for the print to align throughout. To achieve this, fold each fabric wedge template in half and mark the fold line; align the center fold line either with the design or at right angles to the direction of the design, depending on the print; and then mark and cut fabric.

Fold.

Finding wedge center

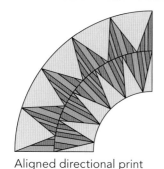

Aligned directional print

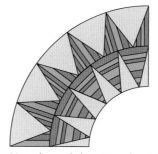

Not aligned directional print

Preparing Templates

Prepare templates from the patterns as described below.

FREEZER-PAPER TEMPLATES

All patterns are the finished size.

> *The seam allowance needs to be added when cutting the fabric.*

Freezer-paper templates are recommended since, once ironed to the fabric, they prevent slipping for the curved edges, and they may be reused.

Patterns do not need to be reversed.

1. Using a ruler and mechanical pencil, trace Patterns A–P (pullout page P1) onto the dull side of freezer paper.

2. Label each template and carefully cut along the lines.

3. Fold the template into quarters and mark matching points. For the larger templates, fold into eighths and mark matching points.

4. With a dry iron, press the template pieces to the *wrong side* of the fabric, leaving ½″ between pieces for the seam allowance.

5. If possible, cut the straight sides of all plain sections parallel to the fabric edges to minimize distortion. Alternately, starch the fabric before cutting.

6. When cool, using a mechanical pencil or a Pigma pen, trace around the edge of the template and transfer all matching points to the back of the arc. These are the sewing lines. Take care not to distort the fabric.

7. To prevent stretching the fabric, use a sandpaper board base and mechanical pencil to trace around the freezer-paper template.

8. Add a seam allowance to all sides, ¼˝ from curved sides and ½˝ from straight sides of each template.

9. Using fabric scissors, cut the fabric just outside the marked lines.

Trace around the template, add a seam allowance, and cut.

FOUNDATION PAPERS OR VILENE FOR THE PIECED ARCS

1. Tape together enough light-weight paper to completely cover each separate arc. Several arcs may be cut from the same piece of paper, but they must not overlap.

2. No seam allowance is indicated on the pattern. A ¼˝ seam allowance needs to be added. Trace all pieced arcs onto the lightweight paper with a mechanical pencil, leaving 1˝ between the arcs.

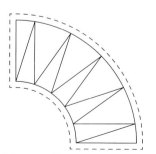

Add seam allowance to pattern.

3. Number each area on the foundation as shown. The numbers indicate the piecing order. The marked side is your sewing side and the reverse side is where your fabric will go, with the wrong side of the fabric against the paper.

4. On each arc, also include the block name and arc size as shown on the pattern. This is useful if the arcs become mixed or if you want to swap arcs later.

5. Carefully cut ⅛˝ beyond the added seam allowance line with craft scissors.

6. Place in labeled resealable bags.

FABRIC TEMPLATES

For foundation piecing, the fabric needs to be cut with a ½˝ seam allowance to ensure the section is covered entirely when piecing.

1. Trace each different wedge once, leaving 1˝ between the pieces.

2. Add a ½˝ seam allowance to all sides.

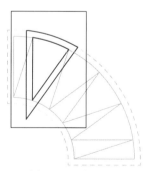

Add seam allowance.

3. Trim sharp triangle points to only ½˝ beyond the point. Place a ruler parallel to the bottom of the triangle and measure ½˝ beyond the point. Trim.

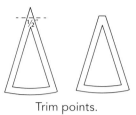

Trim points.

4. Write the cutting information on the template, and cut along the outer line.

Write information on template.

5. Cut a strip of fabric the width of the tallest pattern piece. From the strip, cut the pieces as required, rotating the pieces along the strip and including the seam allowance. Fabric requirements allow for one extra wedge to be cut on every strip.

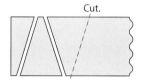

Rotate templates when cutting.

6. For some of the blocks, rectangles are used to cover very narrow wedges and in those cases the size of the cut rectangle is given.

Foundation Piecing

● **Tip: Fabric**

For foundation piecing, the fabric needs to be cut with a ½" seam allowance to ensure the section is covered entirely when pieced.

HOW TO FOUNDATION PIECE

1. On the foundation paper or Vilene, extend all seamlines ¼".

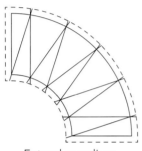

Extend seamlines.

2. Place the Piece 1 fabric on the back (blank side) of the foundation paper, with the wrong side of the fabric against the foundation paper.

3. Hold the paper up to a light source (with the printed design side of the paper facing you) to check that the piece of fabric covers Foundation Piece 1 with at least a ¼" seam allowance on all sides. Pin in place.

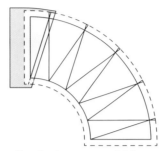

Check placement of fabric.

4. With right sides facing and with the edges aligned, place Piece 2 fabric on Piece 1 fabric. Pin to secure. Fold Fabric 2 back to check that it covers Piece 2. *The narrow end of the fabric must lie within the seam allowance.*

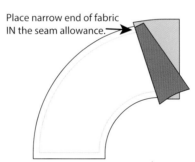

Place narrow end of fabric IN the seam allowance.

Align next fabric edge and place narrow end of fabric carefully.

5. Sew on the line on the foundation paper between Piece 1 and Piece 2, starting and finishing approximately ¼" beyond the seamline. For best results, use a fine machine needle and sew with 12–14 stitches to the inch.

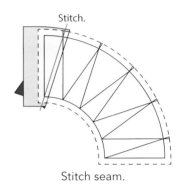

Stitch.

Stitch seam.

6. Finger-press the seam flat. Check that Fabric 2 completely covers Piece 2, with at least a ¼" seam allowance on all sides. If it does not, remove the stitches and resew. Press again with an iron.

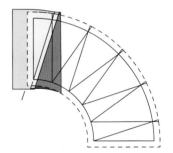

Check that fabric covers Piece 2.

7. Place a bookmark along the next seam. Then fold the paper back, exposing the sewn fabric.

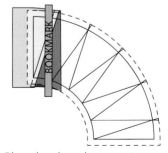

Place bookmark on next seam.

8. Trim only the seam allowance, not the foundation paper, to ¼″ using the Add-a-Quarter ruler.

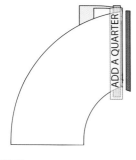

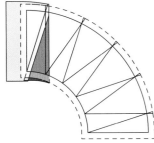

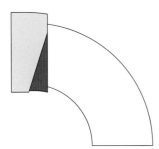

Trim seam allowance to ¼″.

9. Align Fabric 3 to Fabric 2 edge, with the narrow end of the fabric lying within the seam allowance.

10. Continue in the same manner, repeating Steps 4–9, until you have sewn all pieces to the paper.

COMPLETING ARCS WITH SUBUNITS

Some arcs need subunits to be sewn before they are pieced into the main arc. The subunits should be sewn on thin paper, *not* Vilene, as these need to have the paper removed before they are sewn into the main arc.

1. Complete the subunits in the usual manner.

Piece subunit before trimming.

2. Trim each subunit ¼″ from the solid outer line, *only on the marked side.*

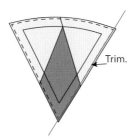

Trim on marked side.

3. Place the Piece 1 fabric in place on the main arc. Baste securely in place. Trim the seam allowance to ¼″. This seam allowance must be accurate.

4. With right sides facing, edges aligned, and junction points matching, place the Piece 2 subunit to the Piece 1 fabric. Pin to secure.

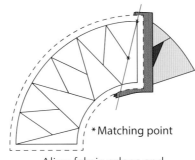

*Matching point

Align fabric edges and intersection points.

5. Using a regular length stitch, baste along the line on the foun-

dation paper between Piece 1 and Piece 2. Check that Subunit 2 completely covers Piece 2, with at least a ¼″ seam allowance on all sides. If it does not, remove the stitches and resew.

NOTE *Seams that were sewn in the subunit are marked with a dotted line on the main arcs. These are* **not** *resewn.*

6. When placement is correct, resew the basted seam using 12–14 stitches to the inch.

7. Remove the foundation papers from the subunit only.

8. Press with an iron.

9. Place a bookmark on the next seam and fold the paper back, exposing the untrimmed edge of the subunit.

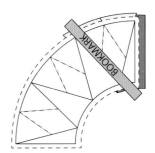

Place bookmark on next seam.

10. Trim only the seam allowance back to ¼″. Do not cut the foundation paper.

11. Continue in the same manner, until you have sewn all pieces to the paper.

12. When complete, trim and mark as for regular foundation piecing.

The Blocks

● **Tips: Organization**

○ *All patterns are finished sizes and do not need to be reversed.*

○ *The wedges at both ends of the arcs should be cut with the outer edge lying parallel to the selvage (on the straight grain) of the fabric.*

○ *After cutting all fabrics for an arc, place them on a flat surface as per the block design to check that you have all the pieces. Pick up the Piece 1 fabric and below that place Piece 2 fabric, then Piece 3 fabric, and so on. All fabric for the arc should be in one pile in the order that it will be used.*

○ *Do not cut the fabric for the plain arc sections until the pieced sections have been completed, and then audition fabric to find one that suits. The appearance of a fabric can change when sewn to different fabric.*

○ *Starch may help to minimize distortion. After applying the starch, wait for a short time for it to dry and then press with a dry iron.*

○ *Sewing through paper will blunt needles a lot faster than regular sewing. Change them as needed, as a blunt needle pierces a larger hole in the fabric.*

○ *All blocks may initially be completed with Pattern P background rather than Pattern Q. This will allow variation for the choice of center corner blocks.*

○ *Highlighting the pattern names and sizes on the pullout pages may help in locating each pattern. Use a different color for each column's patterns.*

Key for Foundation Papers

I = Inner wedge

M = Middle wedge

O = Outer wedge

E = End wedge

ER = End reverse wedge

S = Subunit

G = Geese

W = Wings

A, B, C, D = Wedge and fabric A, B, C, D

Numbers = Piecing order

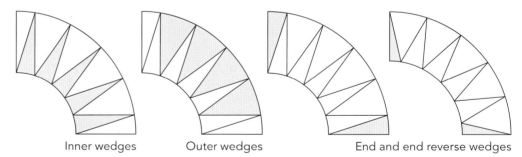

Inner wedges   Outer wedges   End and end reverse wedges

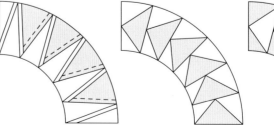

Subunit   Geese   Wings

Completing the Blocks

● *Tip: Swapping Arcs*

Sections may be swapped between blocks. On the edge of each arc is marked the inner and outer arc size. To swap, find an arc with the same measurements and exchange them. Alternately, one arc may be swapped with two or more arcs as long as the final outer arcs are the same size and the inner arcs all match up. For example, a 3″–5″ arc may be swapped with a combined 3″–4″ arc sewn to a 4″–5″ arc.

When sewing a convex curve (the larger side of an inner arc) to a concave curve (the smaller side of an outer arc), it is necessary to ease the convex curve's edge into the edge of the concave curve. However, both seamlines are the same length.

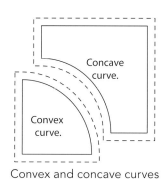

Convex and concave curves

1. Lightly starch the arcs, let them sit for a few minutes, and then press to minimize stretch.

2. Trim both curved sides ¼″ out from the solid outer lines and both straight sides ½″ out from the solid outer lines.

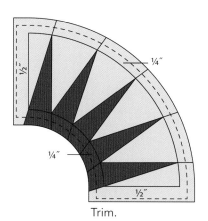

Trim.

3. Carefully remove the papers, taking care not to disturb the stitches. While removing the papers, mark the outer sewing lines and quarter matching points on the back of the fabric using a mechanical pencil. Tweezers may be helpful in removing paper from tight areas.

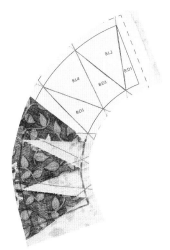

Remove papers and mark.

4. Work with the smaller arcs first, with the convex curve facing up and the concave curve on top, right side down. Pin the 2 adjoining curves together, matching the sewing lines and the matching points while easing sections between these. Place extra pins if needed between these as you ease the 2 fabrics together.

Pin arcs together.

5. Using a thread to match the darker of the 2 fabrics and regular stitch length, stitch carefully along the marked lines; start and finish at the edge of the fabric, beyond the end of the arc.

6. Press away from the arc with the most seams. For some arcs it may help to make small cuts, only in the seam allowance, to allow the seam to change directions along the seam. Take care not to cut the stitching.

Press seam flat.

7. Join all the sections together and then press.

8. Press the block flat with a dry iron.

9. Cut the block square to the largest size possible. No matter how hard we try, often the blocks may be different sizes. It is best to cut to the largest size possible at this stage and trim later to a uniform size. Pin a label to the block with the size.

Patterns

- Copy the foundation patterns from the pullout sheets on Vilene or thin foundation paper, taping together when needed for the larger arcs; add a ¼˝ seam allowance and cut. *All block patterns are on the pullout pages.*

- Prepare freezer-paper templates of each different wedge and *add ½˝ seam allowance* for fabric cutting templates.

- All fabric requirements include an allowance for 1 extra wedge per arc.

- The numbers on the arcs refer to the piecing order. Refer to How to Foundation Piece (page 10).

Bogan Moth (A1)

Unit F
Unit E
Unit D
Unit C
Unit B
Unit A

MATERIALS

Blue print: 4˝ × 4˝

Multicolored stripe: 3˝ × 11¾˝

Pale blue on white: 3˝ × 26¼˝

Green tone-on-tone: 8˝ × 17½˝

Crimson tone-on-tone: 2¼˝ × 23˝

Mustard tone-on-tone: 11˝ × 11˝

Unit	Name	Pattern pullout
A	Pattern A quarter-circle	page P1
B	Foundation B	page P2
C	Foundation E	page P2
D	Pattern K arc	page P1
E	Bogan Moth Unit E	page P3
F	Pattern P	page P1

CUTTING

Blue print: Cut 1 Pattern A for Unit A.

Multicolored stripe: Cut 4 inner, 1 end, and 1 end (rev) wedges of Foundation B for Unit B.

Pale blue on white

- Cut 5 outer wedges of Foundation B for Unit B.

- Cut subcut 4 inner, 1 end, and 1 end (rev) wedges of Foundation E for Unit C.

Green tone-on-tone

- Cut 1 Pattern K arc for Unit D.

- Cut 1 strip 3˝ × 15½˝; subcut 5 outer wedges of Foundation E for Unit C.

- Cut 1 strip 2¼˝ × 13¼˝ and 1 strip 2¼˝ × 8¼˝; subcut 10 inner wedges of Bogan Moth Unit E.

Crimson tone-on-tone: Cut 9 outer, 1 end, and 1 end (rev) wedges of Bogan Moth Unit E.

Mustard tone-on-tone: Cut 1 Pattern P for Unit F.

Crocodile (A2)

 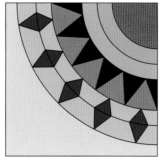

Unit A

Unit B
Unit C

Unit D

Unit E

Unit F
Unit G

MATERIALS

Pink print: 4″ × 4″

Mustard print: 5″ × 5″

Aqua print: 6″ × 6″

Brown-on-black print: 3″ × 14¼″

Orange hand-dyed: 3″ × 15¼″

Mustard tone-on-tone: 2½″ × width of fabric (WOF)

Blue print: 2½″ × 23½″

Pale blue tone-on-tone: 11″ × 11″

Unit	Name	Pattern pullout
A	Pattern A quarter-circle	page P1
B	Pattern C arc	page P1
C	Pattern E arc	page P1
D	Foundation E	page P2
E	Crocodile Unit E	page P5
F	Crocodile Unit F	page P5
G	Pattern P	page P1

CUTTING

Pink print: Cut 1 Pattern A for Unit A.

Mustard print: Cut 1 Pattern C for Unit B.

Aqua print: Cut 1 Pattern E for Unit C.

Brown-on-black print: Cut 4 inner, 1 end, and 1 end (rev) wedges of Foundation E for Unit D.

Orange hand-dyed: Cut 5 outer wedges of Foundation E for Unit D.

Mustard tone-on-tone

- Cut 4 inner, 1 end, and 1 end (rev) wedges of Crocodile Unit E.

- Cut 4 outer, 1 end, and 1 end (rev) wedges of Crocodile Unit F.

Blue print

- Cut 5 inner wedges of Crocodile Unit F.

- Cut 1 strip 2″ × 11½″; subcut 5 outer wedges of Crocodile Unit E.

Pale blue tone-on-tone: Cut 1 Pattern P for Unit G.

● *Tip: Construction Note*

Take extra care with the placement of the trapeziums in Unit E and Unit F. Place these so that there is a similar amount of seam allowance extending on both inner and outer arc before sewing. Pin and fold as before to check that the piece lies correctly.

Platypus (A3)

Unit E

Unit D

Unit C
Unit B

Unit A

MATERIALS

Yellow stripe: 4″ × 4″

Pink print: 5″ × 5″

Green tone-on-tone: 6″ × 6″

Yellow tone-on-tone: 5¼″ × 10½″

Brown print: 5¼″ × 10½″

Cream print: 5¼″ × 22½″

Lilac tone-on-tone: 11″ × 11″

Unit	Name	Pattern pullout
A	Pattern A quarter-circle	page P1
B	Pattern C arc	page P1
C	Pattern E arc	page P1
D	Platypus Unit D	page P5
E	Pattern P	page P1

CUTTING

Yellow stripe: Cut 1 Pattern A for Unit A.

Pink print: Cut 1 Pattern C for Unit B.

Green tone-on-tone: Cut 1 Pattern E for Unit C.

Yellow tone-on-tone: Cut 6 strips 1½″ × 5¼″ for inner A wedges of Platypus Unit D.

Brown print: Cut 6 strips 1½″ × 5¼″ for inner B wedges of Platypus Unit D.

Cream print: Cut 5 outer, 1 end, and 1 end (rev) wedges of Platypus Unit D.

Lilac tone-on-tone: Cut 1 Pattern P for Unit E.

Redback (A4)

 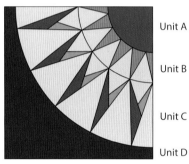

Unit A

Unit B

Unit C

Unit D

Refer to Completing Arcs with Subunits (page 11).

MATERIALS

Green batik: 5¼″ × 14½″

Orange hand-dyed: 3″ × 11¾″

Aqua print: 3″ × 24½″

Mustard print: 3¼″ × 9″

Taupe tone-on-tone: 5¼″ × 20″

Eggplant tone-on-tone: 11″ × 11″

Unit	Name	Pattern pullout
A	Pattern A quarter-circle	page P1
B	Foundation B	page P2
C	Redback Unit C	page P3
C	Redback Subunit	page P2
E	Pattern P	page P1

CUTTING

Green batik

- Cut 1 Pattern A for Unit A.
- Cut 5 strips 1¾″ × 5¼″ for inner wedges of Redback Unit C.

Orange hand-dyed: Cut 4 inner, 1 end, and 1 end (rev) wedges of Foundation B for Unit B.

Aqua print

- Cut 5 outer wedges of Foundation B for Unit B.
- Cut 1 strip 2½″ × 12½″; subcut 5 inner wedges for Redback Subunit for Unit C.

Mustard print: Cut 5 strips 1½″ × 3¼″ for outer wedges of Redback Subunit for Unit C.

Taupe tone-on-tone: Cut 4 outer, 1 end, and 1 end (rev) wedges of Redback Unit C.

Eggplant tone-on-tone: Cut 1 Pattern P for Unit D.

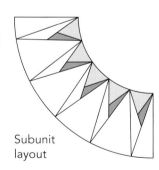

Subunit layout

Brolga (A5)

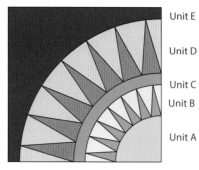

MATERIALS

Yellow with orange spots: 4″ × 4″

Green tone-on-tone: 3″ × 11½″

Pale blue print: 3″ × 16″

Turquoise batik: 7″ × 7″

Pink batik: 4½″ × 14″

Mustard print: 4½″ × 20″

Blue print: 11″ × 11″

Unit	Name	Pattern pullout
A	Pattern A quarter-circle	page P1
B	Brolga Unit B	page P4
C	Pattern I arc	page P1
D	Brolga Unit D	page P2
E	Pattern P	page P1

CUTTING

Yellow with orange spots: Cut 1 Pattern A for Unit A.

Green tone-on-tone: Cut 7 inner wedges of Brolga Unit B.

Pale blue print: Cut 6 outer, 1 end, and 1 end (rev) wedges of Brolga Unit B.

Turquoise batik: Cut 1 Pattern I for Unit C.

Pink batik: Cut 7 inner wedges of Brolga Unit D.

Mustard print: Cut 6 outer, 1 end, and 1 end (rev) wedges of Brolga Unit D.

Blue print: Cut 1 Pattern P for Unit E.

Koala (A6)

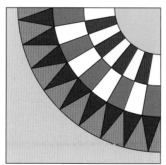

Unit	Name	Pattern pullout
A	Pattern A quarter-circle	page P1
B	Foundation A	page P2
C	Koala Unit C	page P4
D	Foundation K	page P2
E	Pattern P	page P1

MATERIALS

Lime green print: 4″ × 4″

Blue tone-on-tone: 3″ × 7½″

Beige print: 3″ × 9″

Cream print: 3″ × 10″

Navy-gray print: 3″ × 12″

Black-gray print: 3¼″ × 17″

Pink print: 3¼″ × 21¼″

Blue print: 11″ × 11″

CUTTING

Lime green print: Cut 1 Pattern A for Unit A.

Blue tone-on-tone: Cut 4 strips, 1½″ × 3″ for inner wedges of Foundation A for Unit B.

Beige print: Cut 5 strips, 1½″ × 3″ for outer wedges of Foundation A for Unit B.

Cream print: Cut 4 strips, 2″ × 3″ for inner wedges of Koala Unit C.

Navy-gray print: Cut 5 strips, 2″ × 3″ for outer wedges of Koala Unit C.

Black-gray print: Cut 9 inner wedges of Foundation K for Unit D.

Pink print: Cut 8 outer, 1 end, and 1 end (rev) wedges of Foundation K for Unit D.

Blue print: Cut 1 Pattern P for Unit E.

Lyrebird (A7)

Unit E
Unit D
Unit C
Unit B
Unit A

CUTTING

Purple print: Cut 1 Pattern A for Unit A.

Pink print: Cut 6 geese for Lyrebird Unit B.

Pale blue print: Cut 12 wings for Unit B.

Green tone-on-tone: Cut 6 geese for Lyrebird Unit C.

Orange hand-dyed: Cut 12 wings for Lyrebird Unit C.

Maroon with blue stars: Cut 3 A wedges of Lyrebird Unit D.

Teal batik: Cut 3 B wedges of Lyrebird Unit D.

Pale blue on white: Cut 2 outer, 1 end, and 1 end (rev) wedges of Lyrebird Unit D.

Maroon print: Cut 1 Pattern P for Unit E.

MATERIALS

Purple print: 4″ × 4″

Pink print: 3½″ × 11½″

Pale blue print: 2¾″ × 22½″

Green tone-on-tone: 3″ × 19½″

Orange hand-dyed: 2½″ × 29″

Maroon with blue stars: 2¾″ × 14″

Teal batik: 2¾″ × 14″

Pale blue on white: 3¼″ × 22½″

Maroon print: 11″ × 11″

Unit	Name	Pattern pullout
A	Pattern A quarter-circle	page P1
B	Lyrebird Unit B	page P4
C	Lyrebird Unit C	page P4
D	Lyrebird Unit D	page P3
E	Pattern P	page P1

Pelican (A8)

Unit A
Unit B
Unit C
Unit D
Unit E
Unit F

MATERIALS

Yellow stripe: 4″ × 4″

Blue print: 5″ × 5″

Coral batik: 3″ × 16″

Purple batik: 3″ × 14″

White-and-yellow print: 4½″ × 13″

Green tone-on-tone: 4½″ × 35″

White-and-pink print: 3″ × 12″

Purple print: 11″ × 11″

Unit	Name	Pattern pullout
A	Pattern A quarter-circle	page P1
B	Pattern C arc	page P1
C	Foundation D	page P2
D	Foundation G	page P2
E	Foundation M	page P2
F	Pattern P	page P1

CUTTING

Yellow stripe: Cut 1 Pattern A for Unit A.

Blue print: Cut 1 Pattern C for Unit B.

Coral batik: Cut 6 inner, 1 end, and 1 end (rev) wedges of Foundation D for Unit C.

Purple batik: Cut 7 outer wedges of Foundation D for Unit C.

White-and-yellow print: Cut 7 inner wedges of Foundation G for Unit D.

Green tone-on-tone

- Cut 6 outer, 1 end, and 1 end (rev) wedges of Foundation G for Unit D.

- Cut 1 strip 3″ × 15″; subcut 6 inner, 1 end, and 1 end (rev) Foundation M for Unit E.

White-and-pink print: Cut 7 outer wedges of Foundation M for Unit E.

Purple print: Cut 1 Pattern P for Unit F.

Kangaroo (B1)

Unit F
Unit E
Unit D
Unit C
Unit B
Unit A

MATERIALS

Red-black print: 4″ × 4″

Aqua batik: 5″ × 5″

Blue batik: 2¼″ × 13½″

Mustard hand-dyed: 2¼″ × 16″

Dark green print: 7″ × 7″

Red-orange print: 4½″ × 15¼″

Turquoise print: 4½″ × 20¾″

Purple-blue batik: 11″ × 11″

CUTTING

Red-black print: Cut 1 Pattern A for Unit A.

Aqua batik: Cut 1 Pattern B for Unit B.

Blue batik: Cut 8 inner wedges of Kangaroo Unit C.

Mustard hand-dyed: Cut 7 outer, 1 end, and 1 end (rev) wedges of Kangaroo Unit C.

Dark green print: Cut 1 Pattern I, for Unit D.

Red-orange print: Cut 8 inner wedges of Kangaroo Unit E.

Turquoise print: Cut 7 outer, 1 end, and 1 end (rev) wedges of Kangaroo Unit E.

Purple-blue batik: Cut 1 Pattern P for Unit F.

Unit	Name	Pattern pullout
A	Pattern A quarter-circle	page P1
B	Pattern B arc	page P1
C	Kangaroo Unit C	page P3
D	Pattern I arc	page P1
E	Kangaroo Unit E	page P3
F	Pattern P	page P1

Wombat (B2)

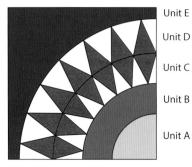

Unit E
Unit D
Unit C
Unit B
Unit A

MATERIALS

Mustard stripe: 4″ × 4″

Green hand-dyed: 6″ × 6″

White tone-on-tone: 3¼″ × 36″

Red tone-on-tone: 3¼″ × 31¼″

Gray-and-black stripe: 11″ × 11″

Unit	Name	Pattern pullout
A	Pattern A quarter-circle	page P1
B	Pattern D arc	page P1
C	Wombat Unit C	page P4
D	Foundation J	page P2
E	Pattern P	page P1

CUTTING

Mustard stripe: Cut 1 Pattern A for Unit A.

Green hand-dyed: Cut 1 Pattern D for Unit B.

White tone-on-tone

- Cut 6 outer, 1 end, and 1 end (rev) wedges of Foundation J for Unit D.
- Cut 1 strip 3″ × 15″; subcut 6 inner, 1 end, and 1 end (rev) wedges of Wombat Unit C.

Red tone-on-tone

- Cut 7 inner wedges of Foundation J for Unit D.
- Cut 1 strip 3″ × 15¾″; subcut 7 outer wedges of Wombat Unit C.

Gray-and-black stripe: Cut 1 Pattern P for Unit E.

Green Tree Frog (B3)

Unit A
Unit B
Unit C
Unit D
Unit E

Unit	Name	Pattern pullout
A	Pattern A quarter-circle	page P1
B	Green Tree Frog Unit B	page P4
C	Green Tree Frog Unit C	page P3
D	Green Tree frog Unit D	page P3
E	Pattern P	page P1

MATERIALS

Blue multicolored print: 4″ × 4″

Purple print: 2″ × 10¾″

Green print: 2″ × 14¼″

Orange print: 2½″ × 9″

Green tone-on-tone: 3¼″ × 7½″

Black-and-gray print: 5″ × 9″

Pink-on-white print: 5″ × 18″

Purple print: 2¼″ × 21½″

Yellow print: 2¼″ × 24″

Beige print: 11″ × 11″

CUTTING

Blue multicolored print: Cut 1 Pattern A for Unit A.

Purple print: Cut 5 inner wedges of Green Tree Frog Unit B.

Green print: Cut 4 outer, 1 end, and 1 end (rev) wedges of Green Tree Frog Unit B.

Orange print: Cut 5 strips, 1½″ × 2½″ for A wedges of Green Tree Frog Unit C.

Green tone-on-tone: Cut 5 strips, 1¼″ × 3¼″ for B wedges of Green Tree Frog Unit C.

Black-and-gray print: Cut 5 strips, 1½″ × 5″ for C wedges of Green Tree Frog Unit C.

Pink-on-white print: Cut 4 outer, 1 end, and 1 end (rev) wedges of Green Tree Frog Unit C.

Purple print: Cut 9 inner, 1 end, and 1 end (rev) wedges of Green Tree Frog Unit D.

Yellow print: Cut 10 outer wedges of Green Tree Frog Unit D.

Beige print: Cut 1 Pattern P for Unit E.

Glider (B4)

	Unit A
	Unit B
	Unit C
	Unit D
	Unit E
	Unit F

MATERIALS

Red-black print: 4″ × 4″

Mustard print: 3″ × 11¾″

Purple batik: 3″ × 12″

Dark blue tone-on-tone: 3″ × 14¼″

Light salmon print: 3″ × 15½″

Orange-on-white print: 2″ × 17¾″

Green batik: 2″ × 17¾″

Purple print: 2¼″ × 18½″

Mustard stripe: 2¼″ × 22″

Pale blue print: 11″ × 11″

Unit	Name	Pattern pullout
A	Pattern A quarter-circle	page P1
B	Foundation B	page P2
C	Foundation E	page P2
D	Foundation I	page P2
E	Foundation L	page P2
F	Pattern P	page P1

CUTTING

Red-black print: Cut 1 Pattern A for Unit A.

Mustard print: Cut 4 inner, 1 end, and 1 end (rev) wedges of Foundation B for Unit B.

Purple batik: Cut 5 outer wedges of Foundation B for Unit B.

Dark blue tone-on-tone: Cut 4 inner, 1 end, and 1 end (rev) wedges of Foundation E for Unit C.

Light salmon print: Cut 5 outer wedges of Foundation E for Unit C.

Orange-on-white print: Cut 4 inner, 1 end, and 1 end (rev) wedges of Foundation I for Unit D.

Green batik: Cut 5 outer wedges of Foundation I for Unit D.

Purple print: Cut 5 inner wedges of Foundation L for Unit E.

Mustard stripe: Cut 4 outer, 1 end, and 1 end (rev) wedges of Foundation L for Unit E.

Pale blue print: Cut 1 Pattern P for Unit F.

Flying Fox (B5)

Unit F
Unit E
Unit D
Unit C
Unit B
Unit A

MATERIALS

Black-and-white stripe: 4″ × 4″

Pink print: 6″ × 6″

Green hand-dyed: 3″ × 14¼″

Red fossil fern: 3″ × 34½″

Deep gold tone-on-tone: 2″ × 22″

Blue tone-on-tone: 10¼″ × 10¼″

Cream print: 11″ × 11″

Unit	Name	Pattern pullout
A	Pattern A quarter-circle	page P1
B	Pattern D arc	page P1
C	Foundation E	page P2
D	Flying Fox Unit D	page P3
E	Pattern M arc	page P1
F	Pattern P	page P1

CUTTING

Black-and-white stripe: Cut 1 Pattern A for Unit A.

Pink print: Cut 1 Pattern D for Unit B.

Green hand-dyed: Cut 4 inner, 1 end, and 1 end (rev) wedges of Foundation E for Unit C.

Red fossil fern

- Cut 5 outer wedges of Foundation E for Unit C.
- Cut 1 strip 2″ × 19″; subcut 10 inner wedges of Flying Fox Unit D.

Deep gold tone-on-tone: Cut 9 outer, 1 end, and 1 end (rev) wedges of Flying Fox Unit D.

Blue tone-on-tone: Cut 1 Pattern M for Unit E.

Cream print: Cut 1 Pattern P for Unit F.

Hairy Nose (B6)

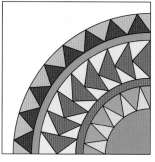

Unit G
Unit F
Unit E
Unit D
Unit C
Unit B
Unit A

Unit	Name	Pattern pullout
A	Pattern A quarter-circle	page P1
B	Hairy Nose Unit B	page P4
C	Pattern G arc	page P1
D	Hairy Nose Unit D	page P4
E	Pattern L arc	page P1
F	Hairy Nose Unit F	page P3
G	Pattern P	page P1

MATERIALS

Yellow-orange print: 4″ × 4″

Pale khaki print: 2½″ × 10″

Green print: 2½″ × 14¾″

Pink print: 6″ × 6″

Multicolored print: 3½″ × 17½″

Blue-on-white print: 2¾″ × 26¼″

Aqua print: 9″ × 9″

Purple print: 2¼″ × 18¼″

Yellow-orange hand-dyed: 2¼″ × 23¼″

Beige print: 11″ × 11″

CUTTING

Yellow-orange print: Cut 1 Pattern A for Unit A.

Pale khaki print: Cut 5 inner wedges of Hairy Nose Unit B.

Green print: Cut 4 outer, 1 end, and 1 end (rev) wedges of Hairy Nose Unit B.

Pink print: Cut 1 Pattern G for Unit C.

Multicolored print: Cut 8 geese for Hairy Nose Unit D.

Blue-on-white print

• Cut 4 squares 2¾″ × 2¾″; subcut across 1 diagonal for 8 half-square triangles for outer wings of Hairy Nose Unit D.

• Cut 1 strip 2½″ × 12½″; subcut 4 squares 2½″ × 2½″; subcut across 1 diagonal for 8 half-square triangles for inner wings of Hairy Nose Unit D.

Aqua print: Cut 1 Pattern L for Unit E.

Purple print: Cut 8 inner wedges of Hairy Nose Unit F.

Yellow-orange hand-dyed: Cut 7 outer, 1 end, and 1 end (rev) wedges of Hairy Nose Unit F.

Beige print: Cut 1 Pattern P for Unit G.

Lizaroo (B7)

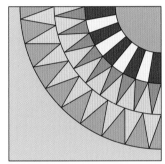

Unit A
Unit B
Unit C
Unit D
Unit E

MATERIALS

Teal batik: 4″ × 4″

Cream print: 3″ × 7½″

Multicolored print: 3″ × 9″

Green hand-dyed: 3″ × 15¼″

Mustard print: 3¼″ × 34¼″

Slate blue batik: 3¼″ × 21¼″

Lime print: 11″ × 11″

Unit	Name	Pattern pullout
A	Pattern A quarter-circle	page P1
B	Foundation A	page P2
C	Foundation F	page P2
D	Foundation K	page P2
E	Pattern P	page P1

CUTTING

Teal batik: Cut 1 Pattern A for Unit A.

Cream print: Cut 4 strips, 1½″ × 3″ for inner wedges of Foundation A for Unit B.

Multicolored print: Cut 5 strips, 1½″ × 3″ for outer wedges of Foundation A for Unit B.

Green hand-dyed: Cut 9 inner wedges of Foundation F for Unit C.

Mustard print

• Cut 9 inner wedges of Foundation K for Unit D.

• Cut 1 strip 3″ × 18¼″; subcut 8 outer, 1 end, and 1 end (rev) wedges of Foundation F for Unit C.

Slate blue batik: Cut 8 outer, 1 end, and 1 end (rev) wedges of Foundation K for Unit D.

Lime print: Cut 1 Pattern P for Unit E.

Fairy Penguin (B8)

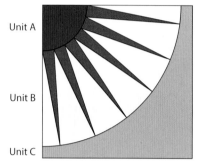

Unit A

Unit B

Unit C

MATERIALS

Dark purple print: 4″ × 4″   Beige print: 7¼″ × 18″

Multicolored stripe: Yellow stripe: 11″ × 11″
7¼″ × 10¼″

Unit	Name	Pattern pullout
A	Pattern A quarter-circle	page P1
B	Fairy Penguin Unit B	page P2
C	Pattern P	page P1

CUTTING

Dark purple print: Cut 1 Pattern A for Unit A.

Multicolored stripe: Cut 6 inner wedges of Fairy Penguin Unit B.

Beige print: Cut 5 outer, 1 end, and 1 end (rev) wedges of Fairy Penguin Unit B.

Yellow stripe: Cut 1 Pattern P for Unit C.

Numbat (C1)

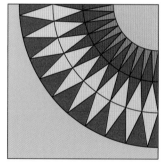

Unit A

Unit B

Unit C

Unit D

Unit E

MATERIALS

Turquoise print: 4″ × 4″   Mustard stripe: 3¼″ × 35¾″

Pink print: 3″ × 14″   Red fossil fern: 3¼″ × 22″

Purple print: 3″ × 34½″   Green print: 11″ × 11″

Unit	Name	Pattern pullout
A	Pattern A quarter-circle	page P1
B	Numbat Unit B	page P3
C	Numbat Unit C	page P3
D	Numbat Unit D	page P3
E	Pattern P	page P1

CUTTING

Turquoise print: Cut 1 Pattern A for Unit A.

Pink print: Cut 10 inner wedges of Numbat Unit B.

Purple print

• Cut 9 outer, 1 end, and 1 end (rev) wedges of Numbat Unit B.

• Cut 9 inner, 1 end, and 1 end (rev) wedges of Numbat Unit C.

Mustard stripe

• Cut 10 inner wedges of Numbat for Unit D.

• Cut 1 strip 3″ × 18″; subcut 10 outer wedges of Numbat for Unit C.

Red fossil fern: Cut 9 outer, 1 end, and 1 end (rev) wedges of Numbat Unit D.

Green print: Cut 1 Pattern P for Unit E.

Lizard (C2)

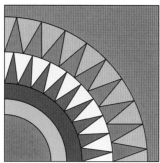

MATERIALS

Orange hand-dyed: 4″ × 4″

Green print: 5″ × 5″

Black-and-white stripe: 6″ × 6″

Green tone-on-tone: 3″ × 15½″

Caramel print: 3″ × 18¼″

Red-orange print: 3¼″ × 17″

Medium blue tone-on-tone: 3¼″ × 21¼″

Coral print: 11″ × 11″

Unit	Name	Pattern pullout
A	Pattern A quarter-circle	page P1
B	Pattern C arc	page P1
C	Pattern E arc	page P1
D	Foundation F	page P2
E	Foundation K	page P2
F	Pattern P	page P1

CUTTING

Orange hand-dyed: Cut 1 Pattern A for Unit A.

Green print: Cut 1 Pattern C for Unit B.

Black-and-white stripe: Cut 1 Pattern E for Unit C.

Green tone-on-tone: Cut 9 inner wedges of Foundation F for Unit D.

Caramel print: Cut 8 outer, 1 end, and 1 end (rev) wedges of Foundation F for Unit D.

Red-orange print: Cut 9 inner wedges of Foundation K for Unit E.

Medium blue tone-on-tone: Cut 8 outer, 1 end, and 1 end (rev) wedges of Foundation K for Unit E.

Coral print: Cut 1 Pattern P for Unit F.

Dugong (C3)

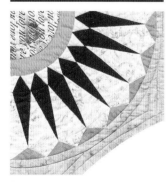

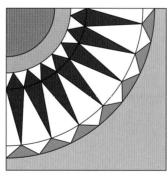

Unit	Name	Pattern pullout
A	Pattern A quarter-circle	page P1
B	Pattern C arc	page P1
C	Foundation D	page P2
D	Foundation G	page P2
E	Foundation M	page P2
F	Pattern P	page P1

MATERIALS

Pink print: 4″ × 4″

Mustard stripe: 5″ × 5″

Very pale green print: 2″ × 16″

Dark blue tone-on-tone: 7″ × 14″

Blue-on-white print: 4½″ × 35″

Teal batik: 3″ × 12″

Lilac batik: 11″ × 11″

CUTTING

Pink print: Cut 1 Pattern A for Unit A.

Mustard stripe: Cut 1 Pattern C for Unit B.

Very pale green print: Cut 6 inner, 1 end, and 1 end (rev) wedges of Foundation D for Unit C.

Dark blue tone-on-tone

- Cut 1 strip 2″ × 14″; subcut 7 outer wedges of Foundation D for Unit C.

- Cut 1 strip 4½″ × 13″; subcut 7 inner wedges of Foundation G for Unit D.

Blue-on-white print

- Cut 6 outer, 1 end, and 1 end (rev) wedges of Foundation G for Unit D.

- Cut 1 strip 3″ × 15″; subcut 4 squares 3″ × 3″ and cut across 1 diagonal for inner, end, and end (rev) wedges of Foundation M for Unit E.

Teal batik: Cut 4 squares 3″ × 3″ and cut across 1 diagonal for outer wedges of Foundation M for Unit E.

Lilac batik: Cut 1 Pattern P for Unit G.

Bluebottle (C4)

Refer to Changing the Center Blocks (page 49).

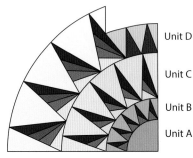

Unit D
Unit C
Unit B
Unit A

MATERIALS

Pink print: 4″ × 4″

Medium blue stripe: 4½″ × WOF

Dark blue tone-on-tone: 12″ × 17″

Dark apricot print: 3″ × 11¾″

Pale blue tone-on-tone: 2¾″ × 12″

Yellow print: 5¼″ × 20″

Pale blue-red print: 3¾″ × 11¼″

Dark blue spots: 5″ × 9″

Pale blue print: 6¼″ × 17″

Dark purple tone-on-tone: 3¾″ × 6½″

Red-orange print: 3¾″ × 8½″

FABRICS

The same dark purple has been used for inner wedges F of Bluebottle Unit D (C4) and also inner wedges B of Magpie Unit G (E4, page 36). Cut the fabric for the Bluebottle first, and then for the Magpie. Total fabric required is 3¾″ × 14½″.

The same red-orange print has been used for outer wedges G of Bluebottle Unit D (C4), inner wedges of Peacock Subunit (D3, page 32), and outer wedges D of Magpie Unit G (E4, page 36). Cut the Bluebottle first, then the Peacock, and finally the Magpie. Total fabric required is 3¾″ × 32″.

Unit	Name	Pattern pullout
A	Pattern A quarter-circle	page P1
B	Bluebottle Unit B	page P6
C	Bluebottle Unit C	page P6
D	Bluebottle Unit D	page P6

CUTTING

Pink print: Cut 1 Pattern A for Unit A.

Medium blue stripe

- Cut 4 strips 2″ × 4¼″ for B wedges of Bluebottle Unit D.

- Cut 1 strip 3½″ × 10½″; subcut 5 strips 1¾″ × 3½″ for B wedges of Bluebottle Unit C.

- Cut 1 strip 2¾″ × 8¼″; subcut 3 squares 2¾″ × 2¾″ and cut across 1 diagonal for A wedges of Bluebottle Unit B.

Dark blue tone-on-tone

- Cut 1 strip 6½″ × 10″; subcut 4 strips 2″ × 6½″ for D wedges of Bluebottle Unit D.

- Cut 1 strip 5½″ × 12″; subcut 5 strips 2″ × 5½″ for C wedges of Bluebottle Unit C.

- Cut 1 strip 3″ × 9″; subcut 5 strips 1½″ × 3″ for B wedges of Bluebottle Unit B.

Dark apricot print: Cut 4 outer, 1 end, and 1 end (rev) wedges of Bluebottle Unit B.

Pale blue tone-on-tone: Cut 5 strips 2″ × 2¾″ for A wedges of Bluebottle Unit C.

Yellow print: Cut 4 outer, 1 end, and 1 end (rev) wedges of Bluebottle Unit C.

Pale blue-red print: Cut 4 strips 2¼″ × 3¾″ for A wedges of Bluebottle Unit D.

Dark blue spots: Cut 4 strips 1¾″ × 5″ for C wedges of Bluebottle Unit D.

Pale blue print: Cut 3 outer, 1 end, and 1 end (rev) wedges of Bluebottle Unit D.

Dark purple tone-on-tone: Cut 2 inner F wedges of Bluebottle Unit D.

Red-orange print: Cut 2 outer G and 1 end wedges of Bluebottle Unit D.

Cassowary (C5)

Unit A
Unit B
Unit C
Unit D
Unit E
Unit F
Unit G
Unit H

Refer to Changing the Center Blocks (page 49).

MATERIALS

Multicolored-on-white print: 4″ × 25½″

Orange-green batik: 2″ × 11¼″

Teal batik: 2″ × 16″

Yellow print: 6″ × 6″

Spotted green print: 3″ × 13″

Black-gray stripe: 3¼″ × 33¼″

Orange tone-on-tone: 6¼″ × 24″

Purple-black print: 11″ × 11″

Red tone-on-tone: 3″ × 9¼″

Lime tone-on-tone: 3″ × 14¼″

Black multicolored: 3¾″ × 22½″

Mustard print: 2¾″ × width of fabric (WOF)

FABRICS

The same lime print has been used for outer wedges C of Cassowary Unit G (C5) and also inner wedges of Subunit and outer wedges of Peacock Too Unit A (D6, page 33). Total fabric required is 4″ × WOF. Cut the fabric for the Peacock Too first.

The Pattern P (pullout page P1) background may be used rather than the Pattern Q (pullout page 1) arc. This will allow for variation when assembling the center section.

Unit	Name	Pattern pullout
A	Pattern A quarter-circle	page P1
B	Cassowary Unit B	page P4
C	Pattern E arc	page P1
D	Cassowary Unit D	page P4
E	Foundation J	page P2
F	Pattern Q arc	page P1
G	Cassowary Unit G	page P6
H	Cassowary Unit H	page P6

CUTTING

Multicolored-on-white print

- Cut 1 Pattern A for Unit A.

- Cut 1 strip 3″ × 21½″; subcut 9 outer D and 1 end wedge of Cassowary Unit G.

Orange-green batik: Cut 7 inner wedges of Cassowary Unit B.

Teal batik: Cut 6 outer, 1 end, and 1 end (rev) wedges of Cassowary for Unit B.

Yellow print: Cut 1 Pattern E for Unit C.

Spotted green print: Cut 7 inner wedges of Cassowary Unit D.

Black-gray stripe

- Cut 7 inner wedges of Foundation J for Unit E.

- Cut 1 strip 3″ × 17¾″; subcut 6 outer, 1 end, and 1 end (rev) wedges of Cassowary Unit D.

Orange tone-on-tone

- Cut 1 strip 3¼″ × 20¾″; subcut 6 outer, 1 end, and 1 end (rev) wedges of Foundation J for Unit E.

- Cut 1 strip 3″ × 24″; subcut 12 inner B wedges of Cassowary Unit G.

Purple-black print: Cut 1 Pattern Q for Unit F.

Red tone-on-tone: Cut 3 inner A wedges of Cassowary for Unit G.

Lime tone-on-tone: Cut 5 outer C wedges of Cassowary for Unit G.

Black multicolored print: Cut 5 squares 3¾″ × 3¾″ and cut across 1 diagonal for geese of Cassowary for Unit H.

Mustard print

- Cut 10 squares 2¾″ × 2¾″ and cut across 1 diagonal for wings of Cassowary Unit H.

- Cut 1 end wedge of Cassowary for Unit H.

Redback Too (C6)

Unit D
Unit C
Unit B
Unit A

Unit	Name	Pattern pullout
A	Pattern A quarter-circle	page P1
B	Foundation C	page P2
C	Redback Subunit	page P2
C	Redback Unit C	page P3
D	Pattern P	page P1

MATERIALS

Pink print: 4″ × 4″

Multicolored stripe: 3″ × 10″

Mustard stripe: 3″ × 27″

Red-black print: 3¼″ × 9″

Dark blue tone-on-tone: 5¼″ × 10½″

Olive green hand-dyed: 5¼″ × 20″

Apricot print: 11″ × 11″

CUTTING

Pink print: Cut 1 Pattern A for Unit A.

Multicolored stripe: Cut 5 inner wedges of Foundation C for Unit B.

Mustard stripe

- Cut 4 outer, 1 end, and 1 end (rev) wedges of Foundation C for Unit B.

- Cut 1 strip 2½″ × 12½″; subcut 5 inner wedges for Redback Subunit.

Red-black print: Cut 5 strips 1½″ × 3¼″ for middle A wedges of Redback Subunit.

Dark blue tone-on-tone: Cut 5 strips 1¾″ × 5¼″ for middle wedges of Redback Unit C.

Olive green hand-dyed: Cut 4 outer, 1 end, and 1 end (rev) wedges of Redback Unit C.

Apricot print: Cut 1 Pattern P for Unit D.

Kingfisher (C7)

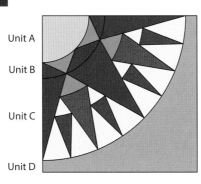

Refer to Completing Arcs with Subunits (page 11).

MATERIALS

Mustard stripe: 4″ × 4″

Peach batik: 2½″ × 12¾″

Blue stripe: 7¾″ × 15½″

Green batik: 2¾″ × 8¾″

Yellow print: 3¾″ × 28½″

Pink-blue batik: 5″ × 7″

Pink-yellow stripe: 11″ × 11″

Unit	Name	Pattern pullout
A	Pattern A quarter-circle	page P1
B	Kingfisher Unit B	page P4
C	Kingfisher Subunit A	page P1
C	Kingfisher Subunit B	page P2
C	Kingfisher Unit C	page P5
D	Pattern P	page P1

CUTTING

Mustard stripe: Cut 1 Pattern A for Unit A.

Peach batik

- Cut 2 inner wedges of Kingfisher Unit B.

- Cut 2 inner wedges of Kingfisher Subunit B.

Blue stripe

- Cut 1 strip 4″ × 7¾″; subcut 1 outer, 1 end, and 1 end (rev) wedges of Kingfisher Unit B.

- Cut 1 strip 6½″ × 11″; subcut 1 inner, 1 end, and 1 end (rev) wedges of Kingfisher Unit C.

Green batik: Cut 4 middle wedges of Kingfisher Subunit A.

Yellow print

- Cut 8 outer wedges of Kingfisher Subunit A.

- Cut 1 strip 2¾″ × 10″; subcut 4 inner wedges of Kingfisher Subunit A.

Pink-blue batik: Cut 2 middle wedges of Kingfisher Subunit B.

Pink-yellow stripe: Cut 1 Pattern P for Unit D.

Construction

Seam allowances are ½˝ unless otherwise noted.

Unit C Assembly

Subunit A

1. Complete 4 of Subunit A.

2. Trim the seam allowance to ¼˝ on the *left side* of 2 subunits only.

3. Trim the seam allowance to ¼˝ on the *right side* of 2 subunits only.

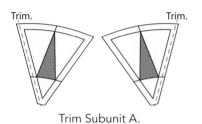

Trim Subunit A.

Subunit B

1. Complete 2 of Subunit B, using a right-trimmed Subunit A for SA:2 and a left-trimmed Subunit A for SA:3.

2. Trim the seam allowance to ¼˝ on the *marked side* of Subunit B.

Placement of Subunit A

Unit C

Complete Unit C, using the trimmed Subunit B for SB:2 and SB:4.

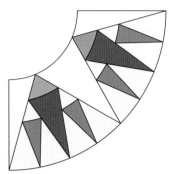

Placement of Subunit B

Possum (C8)

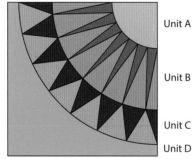

Unit A

Unit B

Unit C

Unit D

MATERIALS

Pale blue print: 4˝ × 4˝

Green print: 5˝ × 11˝

Orange-yellow print: 5˝ × 17½˝

Blue batik: 3¼˝ × 17½˝

Pink print: 3¼˝ × 18¼˝

Pale teal-and-red print: 11˝ × 11˝

Unit	Name	Pattern pullout
A	Pattern A quarter-circle	page P1
B	Possum Unit B	page P4
C	Possum Unit C	page P5
D	Pattern P	page P1

CUTTING

Pale blue print: Cut 1 Pattern A for Unit A.

Green print: Cut 7 inner wedges of Possum Unit B.

Orange-yellow print: Cut 6 outer, 1 end, and 1 end (rev) wedges of Possum Unit B.

Blue batik: Cut 6 inner, 1 end, and 1 end (rev) wedges of Possum Unit C.

Pink print: Cut 7 outer wedges of Possum Unit C.

Pale teal-and-red print: Cut 1 Pattern P for Unit D.

Honeyeater (D1)

 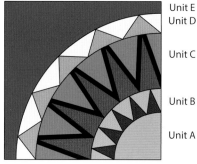

Unit E
Unit D
Unit C
Unit B
Unit A

Refer to Completing Arcs with Subunits (page 11).

MATERIALS

Pink print: 4″ × 4″

Black with gold stars: 2½″ × 10½″

Pale blue tone-on-tone: 2½″ × 15″

Multicolored stripe: 4½″ × 11½″

Black print: 4½″ × 11″

Green print: 3¾″ × 16¼″

Orange with red spots: 2¼″ × 18¼″

Cream print: 2¼″ × 24¾″

Blue print: 11″ × 11″

Unit	Name	Pattern pullout
A	Pattern A quarter-circle	page P1
B	Honeyeater Unit B	page P6
C	Honeyeater Subunit	page P2
C	Honeyeater Unit C	page P5
D	Honeyeater Unit D	page P5
E	Pattern P	page P1

CUTTING

Pink print: Cut 1 Pattern A for Unit A.

Black with gold stars: Cut 5 inner wedges of Honeyeater Unit B.

Pale blue tone-on-tone: Cut 4 outer, 1 end, and 1 end (rev) wedges of Honeyeater Unit B.

Multicolored stripe: Cut 5 inner wedges of Honeyeater Unit C.

Black print

- Cut 4 strips 1″ × 4½″ for middle wedges of Honeyeater Subunit.
- Cut 6 strips 1″ × 4½″ for middle wedges of Honeyeater Unit C.

Green print

- Cut 4 outer wedges for Honeyeater Subunit.
- Cut 1 end and 1 end (rev) wedges of Honeyeater Unit C.

Orange with red spots: Cut 5 inner wedges of Honeyeater Unit D.

Cream print: Cut 4 outer, 1 end, and 1 end (rev) wedges of Honeyeater Unit D.

Blue print: Cut 1 Pattern P for Unit E.

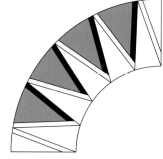

Subunit layout

Wedgetail (D2)

 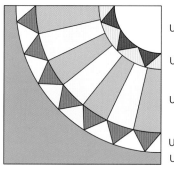

Unit A
Unit B
Unit C
Unit D
Unit E

MATERIALS

Black-and-white stripe: 4″ × 4″

Purple print: 2″ × 10″

Pink-on-white print: 2″ × 14½″

Green print: 5″ × 11″

Lime green tone-on-tone: 5″ × 13¾″

Orange print: 2¼″ × 18¼″

Blue-on-white print: 2¼″ × 22½″

Teal print: 11″ × 11″

Unit	Name	Pattern pullout
A	Pattern A quarter-circle	page P1
B	Wedgetail Unit B	page P4
C	Wedgetail Unit C	page P2
D	Wedgetail Unit D	page P2
E	Pattern P	page P1

CUTTING

Black-and-white stripe: Cut 1 Pattern A for Unit A.

Purple print: Cut 3 inner wedges of Wedgetail Unit B.

Pink-on-white print: Cut 2 outer, 1 end, and 1 end (rev) wedges of Wedgetail Unit B.

Pale green print: Cut 3 strips 2¾″ × 5″ for inner wedges of Wedgetail Unit C.

Lime green tone-on-tone: Cut 4 strips 2¾″ × 5″ for outer wedges of Wedgetail Unit C.

Orange print: Cut 7 inner wedges of Wedgetail Unit D.

Blue-on-white print: Cut 6 outer, 1 end, and 1 end (rev) wedges of Wedgetail Unit D.

Teal print: Cut 1 Pattern P for Unit E.

Peacock (D3)

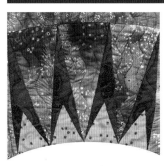

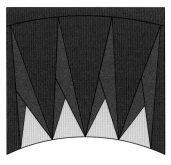

Unit B

Unit A

Refer to Completing Arcs with Subunits (page 11).

MATERIALS

Orange with red spots: 3½″ × 12″

Red-black print: 8½″ × 16¼″

Medium blue print: 10½″ × 18½″

Unit	Name	Pattern pullout
A	Peacock Subunit	page P2
A	Peacock Unit A	page P2
B	Pattern S border	page P1

FABRICS

The same orange with red spot print has been used for inner wedges of the Peacock Subunit (D3), the outer wedges G and E:1 of Bluebottle Unit D (C4, page 26), and the outer wedges D and E:24 of Magpie Unit G (E4, page 36). Cut the fabric for the Bluebottle first, then the Peacock, and then the Magpie. Total fabric required is 3¾″ × 32″.

CUTTING

Orange with red spots: Cut 4 inner wedges of Peacock Subunit.

Red-black print

- Cut 4 strips 2″ × 8½″ for middle wedges of Peacock Unit A.
- Cut 4 middle wedges of Peacock Subunit.

Medium blue print

- Cut 2 strips 2″ × 9″ for end and end (rev) wedges of Peacock Unit A.
- Cut 3 outer wedges of Peacock Unit A.
- Cut 1 Pattern S for Unit B.

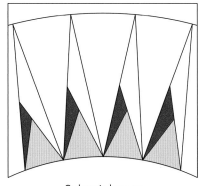

Subunit layout

Peacock Too (D6)

 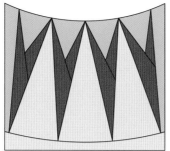

Unit A

Unit B

Refer to Completing Arcs with Subunits (page 11).

MATERIALS

Lime print: 4″ × 21″ **Lemon print:** 10¾″ × 14½″

Purple print: 8½″ × 16″

Unit	Name	Pattern pullout
A	Peacock Subunit	page P2
A	Peacock Unit A	page P2
B	Pattern S border	page P1

FABRICS

The same lime print has been used for the outer wedges C of Cassowary Unit G (C5, page 27) and also the inner wedges of Peacock Too Subunit (D6). Total fabric required is 4″ × WOF. Cut the fabric for the Peacock Too first.

CUTTING

Lime print

- Cut 2 strips 2″ × 9″ for end and end (rev) wedges of Peacock Unit A.
- Cut 1 strip 3½″ × 12″; subcut 4 inner wedges of Peacock Subunit.

Purple print

- Cut 4 strips 2″ × 8½″ for middle wedges of Peacock Unit A.
- Cut 4 middle wedges of Peacock Subunit.

Lemon print

- Cut 3 outer wedges of Peacock Unit A.
- Cut 1 Pattern S for Unit B.

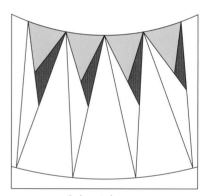

Subunit layout

Blue Whale (D7)

Unit C

Unit B

Unit A

MATERIALS

Multicolored print: 11″ × 11″ **Purple print:** 3¾″ × 24½″

Black-red print: 3¾″ × 15″

Unit	Name	Pattern pullout
A	Pattern H quarter-circle	page P1
B	Blue Whale Unit B	page P4
C	Pattern O	page P1

CUTTING

Multicolored print

- Cut 1 Pattern H for Unit A.
- Cut 1 Pattern O for Unit C.

Black-red print: Cut 4 squares 3¾″ × 3¾″; subcut across 1 diagonal for 7 geese for Blue Whale Unit B.

Purple print: Cut 7 squares 3½″ × 3½″; subcut across 1 diagonal for 14 wings for Blue Whale Unit B.

Possum Too (D8)

Unit A
Unit B
Unit C
Unit D

MATERIALS

Olive and green print: 4″ × 4″

Red hand-dyed: 5″ × 11″

Black with gold stars: 5″ × 17½″

Lemon print: 3¼″ × 17½″

Purple print: 3¼″ × 18¼″

Blue print: 11″ × 11″

CUTTING

Olive and green print: Cut 1 Pattern A for Unit A.

Red hand-dyed: Cut 7 inner wedges of Possum Unit B.

Black with gold stars: Cut 6 outer, 1 end, and 1 end (rev) wedges of Possum Unit B.

Lemon print: Cut 6 inner, 1 end, and 1 end (rev) wedges of Possum Unit C.

Purple print: Cut 7 outer wedges of Possum Unit C.

Blue print: Cut 1 Pattern P for Unit D.

Unit	Name	Pattern pullout
A	Pattern A quarter-circle	page P1
B	Possum Unit B	page P4
C	Possum Unit C	page P5
D	Pattern P	page P1

Galah (E1)

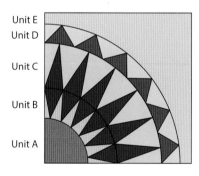

Unit E
Unit D
Unit C
Unit B
Unit A

MATERIALS

Orange hand-dyed: 4″ × 4″

Yellow bubble print: 3″ × 11¾″

Blue stripe: 7½″ × 12¾″

Pale teal print: 4″ × 16¾″

Black and purple print: 2¼″ × 17¾″

Pale green print: 2¼″ × 22″

Yellow tone-on-tone: 11″ × 11″

Unit	Name	Pattern pullout
A	Pattern A quarter-circle	page P1
B	Galah Unit B	page P4
C	Galah Unit C	page P4
D	Galah Unit D	page P4
E	Pattern P	page P1

CUTTING

Orange hand-dyed: Cut 1 Pattern A for Unit A.

Yellow bubble print: Cut 5 inner, 1 end, and 1 end (rev) wedges of Galah Unit B.

Blue stripe

- Cut 1 strip 4″ × 12¼″; subcut 6 inner wedges of Galah Unit C.

- Cut 1 strip 3″ × 12¾″; subcut 6 outer wedges of Galah Unit B.

Pale teal print: Cut 5 outer, 1 end, and 1 end (rev) wedges of Galah Unit C.

Black and purple print: Cut 6 inner wedges of Galah Unit D.

Pale green print: Cut 5 outer, 1 end, and 1 end (rev) wedges of Galah Unit D.

Yellow tone-on-tone: Cut 1 Pattern P for Unit E.

Emu (E2)

Unit E
Unit D
Unit C
Unit B
Unit A

MATERIALS

Orange with red spots: 4″ × 4″

Red-black print: 5″ × 5″

Aqua batik: 6″ × 6″

Dark olive green print: 5¼″ × 14¼″

Medium green print: 5⅜″ × 13½″

Cream print: 4″ × 21½″

Purple-pink print: 11″ × 11″

CUTTING

Orange with red spots: Cut 1 Pattern A for Unit A.

Red-black print: Cut 1 Pattern C for Unit B.

Aqua batik: Cut 1 Pattern E for Unit C.

Dark olive green print: Cut 8 inner wedges of Emu for Unit D.

Medium green print: Cut 8 middle wedges of Emu Unit D.

Cream print: Cut 7 outer, 1 end, and 1 end (rev) wedges of Emu for Unit D.

Purple-pink print: Cut 1 Pattern P for Unit E.

Unit	Name	Pattern pullout
A	Pattern A quarter-circle	page P1
B	Pattern C arc	page P1
C	Pattern E arc	page P1
D	Emu Unit D	page P1
E	Pattern P	page P1

Wallaby (E3)

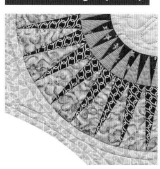
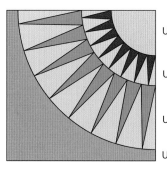

Unit A
Unit B
Unit C
Unit D

MATERIALS

Lilac tone-on-tone: 4″ × 4″

Red with blue print: 3″ × 12¼″

Mustard stripe: 3″ × 15¾″

Blue-and-black print: 5¼″ × 14¼″

Olive green print: 5¼″ × 20½″

Apricot print: 11″ × 11″

Unit	Name	Pattern pullout
A	Pattern A quarter-circle	page P1
B	Wallaby Unit B	page P4
C	Foundation H	page P2
D	Pattern P	page P1

CUTTING

Lilac tone-on-tone: Cut 1 Pattern A for Unit A.

Red with blue print: Cut 8 inner wedges of Wallaby Unit B.

Mustard stripe: Cut 7 outer, 1 end, and 1 end (rev) wedges of Wallaby Unit B.

Blue-and-black print: Cut 8 inner wedges of Foundation H for Unit C.

Olive green print: Cut 7 outer, 1 end, and 1 end (rev) wedges of Foundation H for Unit C.

Apricot print: Cut 1 Pattern P for Unit D.

Magpie (E4)

 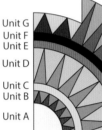

Unit G
Unit F
Unit E

Unit D

Unit C
Unit B

Unit A

Refer to Changing the Center Blocks (page 49).

MATERIALS

Pale blue print: 4″ × 4″

Red-blue batik: 2¼″ × 10½″

Green batik: 2¼″ × 13″

Yellow hand-dyed: 6″ × 6″

Brown-red batik: 4½″ × 12¼″

Blue tone-on-tone: 4½″ × 16¾″

Crimson tone-on-tone: 10½″ × 10½″

Black-gold print: 11″ × 11″

Black-green print: 5½″ × 17¼″

Dark purple tone-on-tone: 3″ × 8″

Lilac print: 5½″ × 20¼″

Orange with red spots: 3″ × 9¼″

FABRICS

The same dark purple has been used for the inner wedges B of Magpie Unit G (E4) and also the inner wedges F of Bluebottle Unit D (C4, page 26). Cut the fabric for the Bluebottle first. Total fabric required is 3¾″ × 14½″.

The same orange with red spots print has been used for the outer wedges G and E:1 of Bluebottle Unit D (C4, page 26), the inner wedges of Peacock Subunit (D3, page 32), and the outer wedges D and E:24 of Magpie Unit G (E4). Cut the fabric for the Bluebottle first, then the Peacock, and then the Magpie. Total fabric required is 3¾″ × 32″.

The Pattern P (pullout page P1) background may be used rather than the Pattern Q (pullout page P1) arc. This will allow for variation when assembling the center section.

Unit	Name	Pattern pullout
A	Pattern A quarter-circle	page P1
B	Magpie Unit B	page P4
C	Pattern F arc	page P1
D	Magpie Unit D	page P3
E	Pattern N arc	page P1
F	Pattern Q arc	page P1
G	Magpie Unit G	page P3

CUTTING

Pale blue print: Cut 1 Pattern A for Unit A.

Red-blue batik: Cut 6 inner wedges of Magpie Unit B.

Green batik: Cut 5 outer, 1 end, and 1 end (rev) wedges of Magpie Unit B.

Yellow hand-dyed: Cut 1 Pattern F for Unit C.

Brown-red batik: Cut 6 inner wedges of Magpie Unit D.

Blue tone-on-tone: Cut 5 outer, 1 end, and 1 end (rev) wedges of Magpie Unit D.

Crimson tone-on-tone: Cut 1 Pattern N for Unit E.

Black-gold print: Cut 1 Pattern Q for Unit F.

Black-green print: Cut 9 inner A wedges of Magpie Unit G.

Dark purple tone-on-tone: Cut 2 inner B wedges of Magpie Unit G.

Lilac print: Cut 8 outer, 1 end, and 1 end (rev) C wedges of Magpie Unit G.

Orange with red spots: Cut 2 outer and 1 end D wedge of Magpie Unit G.

Black Swan (E5)

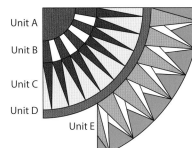

Unit A
Unit B
Unit C
Unit D
Unit E

Refer to Completing Arcs with Subunits (page 11) and Changing the Center Blocks (page 49).

MATERIALS

Red-blue batik: 4″ × 4″

Purple-black print: 3″ × 7½″

Beige batik: 3″ × 9″

Red-black print: 5¼″ × 20″

Caramel-and-multicolored print: 5¼″ × 21¼″

Green batik: 11″ × 11″

Yellow tone-on-tone: 5½″ × 16¼″

White print: 5½″ × 24″

Teal batik: 3½″ × 25″

Unit	Name	Pattern pullout
A	Pattern A quarter-circle	page P1
B	Foundation A	page P2
C	Black Swan Unit C	page P5
D	Pattern Q arc	page P1
E	Black Swan Unit E	page P5
E	Black Swan Subunit	page P3

CUTTING

Red-blue batik: Cut 1 Pattern A for Unit A.

Purple-black print: Cut 5 strips 1½″ × 3″ for outer wedges of Foundation A for Unit B.

Beige batik: Cut 4 strips 1½″ × 3″ for inner wedges of Foundation A for Unit B.

Red-black print: Cut 9 inner wedges of Black Swan Unit C.

Caramel-and-multicolored print: Cut 8 outer, 1 end, and 1 end (rev) wedges of Black Swan Unit C.

Green batik: Cut 1 Pattern Q for Unit D.

Yellow tone-on-tone: Cut 6 inner and 1 end wedge of Black Swan Unit E.

White print

- Cut 6 strips 1¾″ × 5½″ for middle wedges of Black Swan Unit E.

- Cut 1 strip 4¼″ × 10½″; subcut 6 strips 1½″ × 4¼″ for Black Swan Subunit.

Teal batik

- Cut 6 outer wedges of Black Swan Subunit.

- Cut 1 end and 1 end (rev) wedges of Black Swan Unit E.

Subunit layout

FABRICS

The Pattern P (pullout page P1) background may be used initially rather than the Pattern Q (pullout page P1) arc. This will allow for variation when assembling the center section.

One Eye (E6)

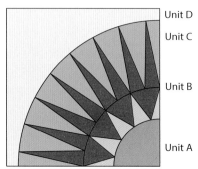

Unit D
Unit C
Unit B
Unit A

MATERIALS

Mustard print: 4″ × 4″

Pale blue tone-on-tone: 3″ × 10″

Red hand-dyed: 8½″ × 14¼″

Green-spotted print: 5¼″ × 20½′

Yellow bubbles print: 11″ × 11″

Unit	Name	Pattern pullout
A	Pattern A quarter-circle	page P1
B	One Eye Unit B	page P6
C	Foundation H	page P2
D	Pattern P	page P1

CUTTING

Mustard print: Cut 1 Pattern A for Unit A.

Pale blue tone-on-tone: Cut 3 inner, 1 end, and 1 end (rev) wedges of One Eye Unit B.

Red hand-dyed

- Cut 1 strip 5¼″ × 14¼″; subcut 8 inner wedges of Foundation H for Unit C.

- Cut 1 strip 3″ × 12″; subcut 4 outer wedges of One Eye Unit B.

Green-spotted print: Cut 7 outer, 1 end, and 1 end (rev) wedges of Foundation H for Unit C.

Yellow bubbles print: Cut 1 Pattern P for Unit D.

Hairy Nose Too (E7)

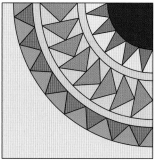

Unit A
Unit B
Unit C
Unit D
Unit E
Unit F
Unit G

Unit	Name	Pattern pullout
A	Pattern A quarter-circle	page P1
B	Hairy Nose Unit B	page P4
C	Pattern G arc	page P1
D	Hairy Nose Unit D	page P4
E	Pattern L arc	page P1
F	Hairy Nose Unit F	page P3
G	Pattern P	page P1

MATERIALS

Multicolored print: 4″ × 4″

Dark green hand-dyed: 2½″ × 10″

White-and-red print: 2½″ × 14¾″

Gold hand-dyed: 9″ × 18½″

Black-and-gray print: 3½″ × 17½″

Crimson print: 2¼″ × 18¼″

Pale blue print: 2¼″ × 23¼″

Pink with stars: 11″ × 11″

CUTTING

Multicolored print: Cut 1 Pattern A for Unit A.

Dark green hand-dyed: Cut 5 inner wedges of Hairy Nose Unit B.

White-and-red print: Cut 4 outer, 1 end, and 1 end (rev) wedges of Hairy Nose Unit B.

Gold hand-dyed

- Cut 1 Pattern L for Unit E.

- Cut 1 Pattern G for Unit C.

- Cut 1 strip 2¾" × 11", subcut 4 squares 2¾" × 2¾"; subcut across 1 diagonal for 8 half-square triangles for outer wings of Hairy Nose Unit D.

- Cut 1 strip 2½" × 12½"; subcut 4 squares 2½" × 2½"; subcut across 1 diagonal for 8 half-square triangles for inner wings of Hairy Nose Unit D.

Black-and-gray print: Cut 8 geese for Hairy Nose Unit D.

Crimson print: Cut 8 inner wedges of Hairy Nose Unit F.

Pale blue print: Cut 7 outer, 1 end, and 1 end (rev) wedges of Hairy Nose Unit F.

Pink with stars: Cut 1 Pattern P for Unit G.

Tasmanian Tiger (E8)

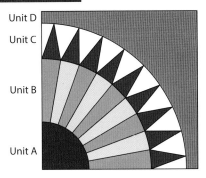

MATERIALS

Dark purple print: 4" × 4"	**Dark blue print:** 3¼" × 17"
Orange print: 5" × 10"	**Cream print:** 3¼" × 21¼"
Pale teal print: 5" × 12"	**Pink batik:** 11" × 11"

Unit	Name	Pattern pullout
A	Pattern A quarter-circle	page P1
B	Tasmanian Tiger Unit B	page P4
C	Foundation K	page P2
D	Pattern P	page P1

CUTTING

Dark purple print: Cut 1 Pattern A for Unit A.

Orange print: Cut 5 strips 2" × 5" for outer wedges of Tasmanian Tiger Unit B.

Pale teal print: Cut 4 strips 2" × 5" for inner wedges of Tasmanian Tiger Unit B.

Dark blue print: Cut 9 inner wedges of Foundation K for Unit C.

Cream print: Cut 8 outer, 1 end, and 1 end (rev) wedges of Foundation K for Unit C.

Pink batik: Cut 1 Pattern P for Unit D.

Bottlenose (F1)

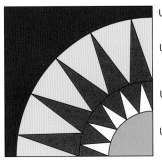

MATERIALS

Lime tone-on-tone: 4" × 4"	**Mustard print:** 5¼" × 20"
White tone-on-tone: 3" × 10"	**Dark purple tone-on-tone:** 11" × 11"
Red-black print: 8½" × 14½"	

Unit	Name	Pattern pullout
A	Pattern A quarter-circle	page P1
B	Foundation C	page P2
C	Bottlenose Unit C	page P4
D	Pattern P	page P1

CUTTING

Lime tone-on-tone: Cut 1 Pattern A for Unit A.

White tone-on-tone: Cut 5 inner wedges of Foundation C for Unit B.

Red-black print

- Cut 1 strip 5¼″ × 12¼″; subcut 5 inner wedges of Bottlenose Unit C.

- Cut 1 strip 3″ × 14½″; subcut 4 outer, 1 end, and 1 end (rev) wedges of Foundation C for Unit B.

Mustard print: Cut 4 outer, 1 end, and 1 end (rev) wedges of Bottlenose Unit C.

Dark purple tone-on-tone: Cut 1 Pattern P for Unit D.

Bilby (F2)

Unit F	
Unit E	
Unit D	
Unit C	
Unit B	
Unit A	

MATERIALS

Mustard print: 4″ × 4″

Teal print: 5″ × 5″

White print: 2″ × 14¾″

Blue print: 2″ × 15¾″

Spotted blue print: 4¼″ × 14½″

Orange with red spots: 4¼″ × 18½″

Olive hand-dyed: 2″ × 28″

Red hand-dyed: 2″ × 32½″

Black-and-blue chain print: 11″ × 11″

Unit	Name	Pattern pullout
A	Pattern A quarter-circle	page P1
B	Pattern C arc	page P1
C	Bilby Unit C	page P6
D	Bilby Unit D	page P3
E	Bilby Unit E	page P3
F	Pattern P	page P1

CUTTING

Mustard print: Cut 1 Pattern A for Unit A.

Teal print: Cut 1 Pattern C for Unit B.

White print: Cut 7 inner, 1 end, and 1 end (rev) wedges of Bilby Unit C.

Blue print: Cut 8 outer wedges of Bilby Unit C.

Spotted blue print: Cut 8 inner wedges of Bilby Unit D.

Orange with red spots: Cut 7 outer, 1 end, and 1 end (rev) wedges of Bilby Unit D.

Olive hand-dyed: Cut 16 inner wedges of Bilby Unit E.

Red hand-dyed: Cut 15 outer, 1 end, and 1 end (rev) wedges of Bilby Unit E.

Black-and-blue chain print: Cut 1 Pattern P for Unit F.

Frillneck (F3)

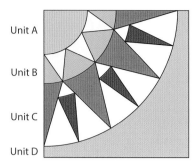

Unit A
Unit B
Unit C
Unit D

Refer to Completing Arcs with Subunits (page 11).

MATERIALS

Mustard stripe: 4″ × 4″

Blue-on-white print: 3″ × 8½″

Multicolored stripe: 3″ × 15″

Orange hand-dyed: 5¼″ × 13¾″

Purple print: 4¼″ × 7¼″

Cream print: 4½″ × 23″

Blue-green print: 11″ × 11″

Unit	Name	Pattern pullout
A	Pattern A quarter-circle	page P1
B	Frillneck Unit B	page P2
C	Frillneck Unit C	page P4
C	Frillneck Subunit	page P1
D	Pattern P	page P1

CUTTING

Mustard stripe: Cut 1 Pattern A for Unit A.

Blue-on-white print: Cut 3 inner wedges of Frillneck Unit B.

Multicolored stripe: Cut 2 outer, 1 end, and 1 end (rev) wedges of Frillneck Unit B.

Orange hand-dyed: Cut 2 inner, 1 end, and 1 end (rev) wedges of Frillneck Unit C.

Purple print: Cut 3 middle wedges of Frillneck Subunit.

Cream print

- Cut 3 outer wedges of Frillneck Subunit.

- Cut 3 outer wedges of Frillneck Unit C.

- Cut 2 strips 2″ × 5″; subcut 3 inner wedges of Frillneck Subunit.

Blue-green print: Cut 1 Pattern P for Unit D.

Subunit layout

Bandicoot (F4)

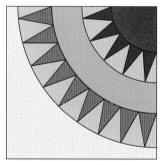

Unit A
Unit B
Unit C
Unit D
Unit E

Unit	Name	Pattern pullout
A	Pattern A quarter-circle	page P1
B	Foundation C	page P2
C	Pattern J arc	page P1
D	Foundation K	page P2
E	Pattern P	page P1

MATERIALS

Red-black print: 4″ × 4″

Blue batik: 3″ × 10″

Mustard stripe: 3″ × 14½″

Green-spotted print: 8″ × 8″

Pink batik: 3¼″ × 17″

Blue tone-on-tone: 3¼″ × 21¼″

Red-on-white print: 11″ × 11″

CUTTING

Red-black print: Cut 1 Pattern A for Unit A.

Blue batik: Cut 5 inner wedges of Foundation C for Unit B.

Mustard stripe: Cut 4 outer, 1 end, and 1 end (rev) wedges of Foundation C for Unit B.

Green-spotted print: Cut 1 Pattern J for Unit C.

Pink batik: Cut 9 inner wedges of Foundation K for Unit D.

Blue tone-on-tone: Cut 8 outer, 1 end, and 1 end (rev) wedges of Foundation K for Unit D.

Red-on-white print: Cut 1 Pattern P for Unit E.

Ghost Bat (F5)

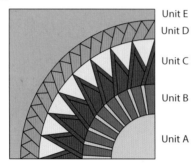

Unit E
Unit D
Unit C
Unit B
Unit A

Refer to Completing Arcs with Subunits (page 11).

MATERIALS

Aqua print: 4″ × 4″

Yellow print: 3″ × 13½″

Dark green tone-on-tone: 3″ × 9″

Purple print: 3¼″ × 19″

Red print: 41/14″ × 17″

Pale blue print: 3¼″ × 18″

Orange-and-green batik: 2½″ × 31½″

Blue batik: 21/12″ × 22½″

Pink print: 11″ × 11″

Unit	Name	Pattern pullout
A	Pattern A quarter-circle	page P1
B	Ghost Bat Unit B	page P4
C	Ghost Bat Subunit	page P4
C	Ghost bat Unit C	page P5
D	Foundation N	page P2
E	Pattern P	page P1

CUTTING

Aqua print: Cut 1 Pattern A for Unit A.

Yellow print: Cut 8 strips 1″ × 3″ for inner wedges of Ghost Bat Unit B.

Dark green tone-on-tone: Cut 8 strips 1½″ × 3″ for outer wedges of Ghost Bat Unit B.

Purple print

- Cut 7 inner wedges of Ghost Bat Subunit.
- Cut 1 end and 1 end (rev) wedge of Ghost Bat 5 Unit C.

Red print

- Cut 7 strips 1″ × 4¼″ for middle wedges of Ghost Bat Subunit.
- Cut 9 strips 1″ × 4¼″ for middle wedges of Ghost Bat Unit C.

Pale blue print: Cut 8 outer wedges of Ghost Bat Unit C.

Orange-and-green batik: Cut 17 strips 1¾″ × 2½″ for inner wedges of Foundation N, for Unit D.

Blue batik: Cut 8 squares 2½″ × 2½″; subcut across 1 diagonal for 16 outer wedges of Foundation N for Unit D.

Pink print: Cut 1 Pattern P for Unit E.

Subunit layout

Fruit Bat (F6)

MATERIALS

Orange batik: 4″ × 4″

Green-purple batik: 1¾″ × 15″

Brown print: 1¾″ × 15″

Pink print: 5¼″ × 10″

Blue batik: 5¼″ × 10″

Mustard print: 5¼″ × 17¾″

Pale aqua tone-on-tone: 11″ × 11″

Unit	Name	Pattern pullout
A	Pattern A quarter-circle	page P1
B	Fruit Bat Unit B	page P3
C	Fruit Bat Unit C	page P3
D	Pattern P	page P1

CUTTING

Orange batik: Cut 1 Pattern A for Unit A.

Green-purple batik: Cut 4 strips 1¾″ × 3″ for inner wedges of Fruit Bat Unit B.

Brown print: Cut 4 strips 1¾″ × 3″ for outer wedges of Fruit Bat Unit B.

Pink print: Cut 4 strips 2″ × 5¼″ for inner A wedges of Fruit Bat Unit C.

Blue batik: Cut 4 strips 2″ × 5¼″ for inner B wedges of Fruit Bat Unit C.

Mustard print: Cut 3 outer, 1 end, and 1 end (rev) wedges of Fruit Bat Unit C.

Pale aqua tone-on-tone: Cut 1 Pattern P for Unit D.

Koala Too (F7)

  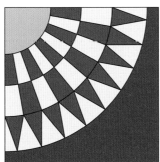

MATERIALS

Lime green print: 4″ × 4″

Caramel print: 3¼″ × 38″

Navy blue print: 3¼″ × 34″

Red-and-black print: 11″ × 11″

Unit	Name	Pattern pullout
A	Pattern A quarter-circle	page P1
B	Foundation A	page P2
C	Koala Unit C	page P4
D	Foundation K	page P2
E	Pattern P	page P1

CUTTING

Lime green print: Cut 1 Pattern A for Unit A.

Caramel print

- Cut 8 outer, 1 end, and 1 end (rev) wedges of Foundation K for Unit D.

- Cut 1 strip 3″ × 19½″; subcut 4 strips 1½″ × 3″ for inner wedges of Foundation A for Unit B and 5 strips 2″ × 3″ for outer wedges of Koala Unit C.

Navy blue print

- Cut 9 inner wedges of Foundation K for Unit D.

- Cut 1 strip 3″ × 19½″; subcut 5 strips 1½″ × 3″ for outer wedges of Foundation A for Unit B and 4 strips 2″ × 3″ for inner wedges of Koala Unit C.

Red-and-black print: Cut 1 Pattern P for Unit E.

Echidna (F8)

Unit A
Unit B
Unit C
Unit D
Unit E

MATERIALS

Black-and-gold print: 4″ × 4″

Red-black print: 5″ × 5″

Dark purple tone-on-tone: 6″ × 6″

Brown print: 5½″ × 24″

Cream print: 5½″ × 34″

Dark purple print: 11″ × 11″

Unit	Name	Pattern pullout
A	Pattern A quarter-circle	page P1
B	Pattern C arc	page P1
C	Pattern E arc	page P1
D	Echidna Unit D	page P2
E	Pattern P	page P1

CUTTING

Black-and-gold print: Cut 1 Pattern A for Unit A.

Red-black print: Cut 1 Pattern C for Unit B.

Dark purple tone-on-tone: Cut 1 Pattern E for Unit C.

Brown print: Cut 15 strips 1½″ × 5½″ for inner wedges of Echidna Unit D.

Cream print: Cut 16 strips 2″ × 5½″ for outer wedges of Echidna Unit D.

Dark purple print: Cut 1 Pattern P for Unit E.

Jellyfish (G1)

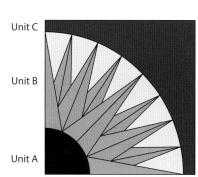

Unit C
Unit B
Unit A

MATERIALS

Black frog print: 4″ × 4″

Lilac print: 7½″ × 14½″

Blue-green stripe: 7½″ × 14½″

Blue-on-white print: 4¼″ × 18½″

Blue print: 11″ × 11″

Unit	Name	Pattern pullout
A	Pattern A quarter-circle	page P1
B	Jellyfish Subunit A	page P3
B	Jellyfish Subunit B	page P3
B	Jellyfish Unit B	page P6
C	Pattern P	page P1

CUTTING

Black frog print: Cut 1 Pattern A for Unit A.

Lilac print

- Cut 2 tall A wedges for Subunit B, 1 tall and 1 end A wedges for Jellyfish Unit B.

- Cut 1 strip 4½″ × 7″; subcut 2 short A wedges for Subunit A and 2 short A wedges for Subunit B.

Blue-green stripe

- Cut 2 tall B wedges for Subunit A, 1 tall and 1 end (rev) B wedges for Jellyfish Unit B.

- Cut 1 strip 4½″ × 7″; subcut 2 short B wedges for Subunit A and 2 short B wedges for Subunit B.

Blue-on-white print

- Cut 4 outer wedges for Subunit A.

- Cut 4 outer wedges for Subunit B.

Blue print: Cut 1 Pattern P for Unit C.

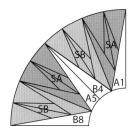

Subunit layout

Cuttlefish (G2)

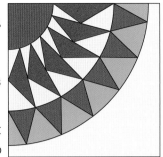

Unit A
Unit B
Unit C
Unit D

CUTTING

Lilac and star print: Cut 1 Pattern A for Unit A.

Red tone-on-tone: Cut 6 geese for Cuttlefish Unit B.

Cream print: Cut 12 wings for Cuttlefish Unit B.

Gray-black check: Cut 6 inner wedges of Cuttlefish Unit C.

Teal print: Cut 5 outer, 1 end, and 1 end (rev) wedges of Cuttlefish Unit C.

Cream print: Cut 1 Pattern P for Unit D.

MATERIALS

Lilac and star print: 4″ × 4″

Red tone-on-tone: 4½″ × 18½″

Cream print: 3¾″ × 26¼″

Gray-black check: 3¼″ × 15¼″

Teal print: 3¼″ × 19½″

Cream print: 11″ × 11″

Unit	Name	Pattern pullout
A	Pattern A quarter-circle	page P1
B	Cuttlefish Unit B	page P4
C	Cuttlefish Unit C	page P3
D	Pattern P	page P1

Sea Dragon (G3)

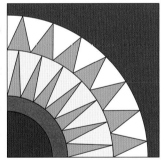

Unit E
Unit D
Unit C
Unit B
Unit A

CUTTING

Blue print: Cut 1 Pattern A for Unit A.

Red print: Cut 1 Pattern C for Unit B.

Teal batik: Cut 7 inner wedges of Sea Dragon Unit C.

Cream print: Cut 6 outer, 1 end, and 1 end (rev) wedges of Sea Dragon Unit C.

Teal print: Cut 7 inner wedges of Foundation J for Unit D.

White tone-on-tone: Cut 6 outer, 1 end, and 1 end (rev) wedges of Foundation J for Unit D.

Maroon and blue stars: Cut 1 Pattern P for Unit E.

MATERIALS

Blue print: 4″ × 4″

Red print: 5″ × 5″

Teal batik: 4″ × 12¼″

Cream print: 4″ × 17½″

Teal print: 3¼″ × 15½″

White tone-on-tone: 3¼″ × 20¾″

Maroon and blue stars: 11″ × 11″

Unit	Name	Pattern pullout
A	Pattern A quarter-circle	page P1
B	Pattern C arc	page P1
C	Sea Dragon Unit C	page P6
D	Foundation J	page P2
E	Pattern P	page P1

Pipistrelle (G4)

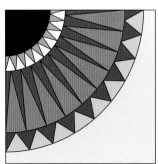

Unit A
Unit B
Unit C
Unit D
Unit E

MATERIALS

Black-and-gold print: 4″ × 4″

Green print: 2″ × 15¼″

Lemon print: 2″ × 14¾″

Purple print: 5″ × 16½″

Red-and-orange stripe: 5″ × 18″

Blue print: 2¼″ × 22″

Mustard stripe: 2¼″ × 21½″

Aqua tone-on-tone: 11″ × 11″

Unit	Name	Pattern pullout
A	Pattern A quarter-circle	page P1
B	Pipistrelle Unit B	page P4
C	Pipistrelle Unit C	page P6
D	Pipistrelle Unit D	page P6
E	Pattern P	page P1

CUTTING

Black-and-gold print: Cut 1 Pattern A for Unit A.

Green print: Cut 8 inner, 1 end, and 1 end (rev) wedges of Pipistrelle Unit B.

Lemon print: Cut 9 outer wedges of Pipistrelle Unit B.

Purple print: Cut 10 strips 1½″ × 5″ for inner wedges of Pipistrelle Unit C.

Red-and-orange stripe: Cut 9 outer wedges of Pipistrelle Unit C.

Blue print: Cut 8 inner, 1 end, and 1 end (rev) wedges of Pipistrelle Unit D.

Mustard stripe: Cut 9 outer wedges of Pipistrelle Unit D.

Aqua tone-on-tone: Cut 1 Pattern P for Unit E.

Emu Too (G5)

Unit D
Unit C
Unit B
Unit A

MATERIALS

Black with mustard stars: 4″ × 4″

Teal batik: 6″ × 6″

Black with brown print: 5¼″ × 14¼″

Brown print: 5⅜″ × 13½″

Cream print: 4″ × 21½″

Green print: 11″ × 11″

Unit	Name	Pattern pullout
A	Pattern A quarter-circle	page P1
B	Pattern D arc	page P1
C	Emu Unit D	page P1
D	Pattern P	page P1

CUTTING

Black with mustard stars: Cut 1 Pattern A for Unit A.

Teal batik: Cut 1 Pattern D for Unit B.

Black with brown print: Cut 8 inner wedges of Emu Unit D for Unit C.

Brown print: Cut 8 middle wedges of Emu Unit D for Unit C.

Cream print: Cut 7 outer, 1 end, and 1 end (rev) wedges of Emu Unit D for Unit C.

Green print: Cut 1 Pattern P for Unit D.

Dingo (G6)

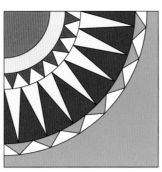

Unit A
Unit B
Unit C
Unit D
Unit E
Unit F

MATERIALS

Ochre print: 4″ × 4″

Cream multicolored print: 5″ × 5″

Red-black print: 2″ × 14½″

White print: 2″ × 16½″

Ecru print: 4½″ × 13″

Blue print: 4½″ × 20″

Orange with red spots: 2¼″ × 21″

Cream print: 2¼″ × 23¾″

Teal print: 11″ × 11″

Unit	Name	Pattern pullout
A	Pattern A quarter-circle	page P1
B	Pattern C arc	page P1
C	Dingo Unit C	page P4
D	Foundation G	page P2
E	Dingo Unit E	page P3
F	Pattern P	page P1

CUTTING

Ochre print: Cut 1 Pattern A for Unit A.

Cream multicolored print: Cut 1 Pattern C for Unit B.

Red-black print: Cut 7 inner wedges of Dingo Unit C.

White print: Cut 6 outer, 1 end, and 1 end (rev) wedges of Dingo Unit C.

Ecru print: Cut 7 inner wedges of Foundation G for Unit D.

Blue print: Cut 6 outer, 1 end, and 1 end (rev) wedges of Foundation G for Unit D.

Orange with red spots: Cut 7 inner wedges of Dingo Unit E.

Cream print: Cut 6 outer, 1 end, and 1 end (rev) wedges of Dingo Unit E.

Teal print: Cut 1 Pattern P for Unit F.

Sheathtail Bat (G7)

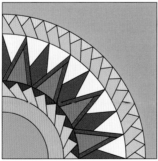

Unit F
Unit E
Unit D
Unit C
Unit B
Unit A

Unit	Name	Pattern pullout
A	Pattern A quarter-circle	page P1
B	Pattern C arc	page P1
C	Sheathtail Bat Unit C	page P4
D	Sheathtail Bat Subunit A	page P2
D	Sheathtail Bat Subunit B	page P2
D	Sheathtail Bat Unit D	page P2
E	Foundation N	page P2
F	Pattern P	page P1

Refer to Completing Arcs with Subunits (page 11).

MATERIALS

Blue and teal batik: 4″ × 4″

Lilac tone-on-tone: 5″ × 5″

Orange with red spots: 2½″ × 15″

Blue print: 2½″ × 12¼″

Purple print: 3¼″ × 9¾″

Red hand-dyed: 4″ × 9″

Green print: 4″ × 11½″

Yellow print: 3″ × 17½″

Teal batik: 2½″ × 31½″

Purple print: 2½″ × 22½″

Orange-and-yellow print: 11″ × 11″

CUTTING

Blue and teal batik: Cut 1 Pattern A for Unit A.

Lilac tone-on-tone: Cut 1 Pattern C for Unit B.

Orange with red spots: Cut 9 strips 1½″ × 2½″ for inner wedges of Sheathtail Bat Unit C.

Blue print: Cut 4 squares 2½″ × 2½″; subcut across 1 diagonal for 8 outer wedges of Sheathtail Bat Unit C.

Purple print: Cut 4 inner wedges for Subunit A.

Red hand-dyed

- Cut 4 strips 1″ × 4″ for Subunit A.

- Cut 4 strips 1″ × 4″ for middle wedges of Sheathtail Bat Unit D.

Green print

- Cut 4 inner wedges for Subunit B.

- Cut 1 end and 1 end (rev) wedges of Sheathtail Bat Unit D.

Yellow print

- Cut 4 outer wedges for Subunit B.

- Cut 4 outer wedges of Sheathtail Bat Unit D.

Teal batik: Cut 17 strips 1¾″ × 2½″ for inner wedges of Foundation N for Unit E.

Purple print: Cut 8 squares 2½″ × 2½″; subcut across 1 diagonal for 16 outer wedges of Foundation N for Unit E.

Orange-and-yellow print: Cut 1 Pattern P for Unit F.

Construction

Seam allowances are ¼″ unless otherwise noted.

Unit C Assembly

1. Complete all subunits.

2. Complete Sheathtail Bat Unit D, using a complete Subunit B for SB:17.

3. Trim the seam allowance on SB:17 to ½″ on the end as usual.

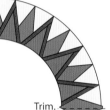

Trim.

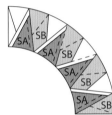

Trim SB:17   Subunit placement

Glider Too (G8)

Unit A
Unit B
Unit C
Unit D
Unit E
Unit F

MATERIALS

Red hand-dyed: 4″ × 4″

Purple-pink print: 3″ × 12″

Dark blue tone-on-tone: 3″ × 12″

Green hand-dyed: 3″ × 14¼″

Blue-pink batik: 3″ × 15½″

Yellow batik: 2¼″ × 36″

Aqua batik: 2¼″ × width of fabric (WOF)

Purple print: 11″ × 11″

Unit	Name	Pattern pullout
A	Pattern A quarter-circle	page P1
B	Foundation B	page P2
C	Foundation E	page P2
D	Foundation I	page P2
E	Foundation L	page P2
F	Pattern P	page P1

CUTTING

Red hand-dyed: Cut 1 Pattern A for Unit A.

Purple-pink print: Cut 4 inner, 1 end, and 1 end (rev) wedges of Foundation B for Unit B.

Dark blue tone-on-tone: Cut 5 outer wedges of Foundation B for Unit B.

Green hand-dyed: Cut 4 inner, 1 end, and 1 end (rev) wedges of Foundation E for Unit C.

Blue-pink batik: Cut 5 outer wedges of Foundation E for Unit C.

Yellow batik

- Cut 4 outer, 1 end, and 1 end (rev) wedges of Foundation L for Unit E.

- Cut 1 strip 2″ × 19″; subcut 4 inner, 1 end, and 1 end (rev) wedges of Foundation I for Unit D.

Aqua batik

- Cut 5 inner wedges of Foundation L for Unit E.

- Cut 1 strip 2″ × 18″; subcut 5 outer wedges of Foundation I for Unit D.

Purple print: Cut 1 Pattern P for Unit F.

Assembling the Quilt

Trimming the Blocks

All blocks must be the same size for the quilt to lie flat.

1. Using a 12½˝ square rotary cutting ruler, trim both sides beside the 3˝ quarter-circle on all blocks.

Care needs to be taken with the cutting, ensuring that a ¼˝ seam allowance remains beyond the end of the design section.

The first arc should lie on the 3¼˝ mark, while the outer arc should lie on the 9½˝ mark.

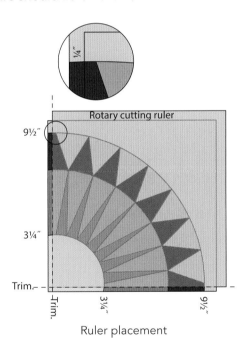

Ruler placement

2. After trimming the 2 inner sides on all blocks, find the smallest block.

3. Trim the remaining 2 sides to make it square. Record this measurement.

4. Trim all blocks to the same size. Part of a wedge might be trimmed off at this time, and you might lose a point or two.

Center Unit

TEMPLATE PREPARATION

Prepare templates from Patterns P, Q, R, S, and T (pullout page P1), using freezer paper.

CHANGING THE CENTER BLOCKS

The Cassowary (C5, page 27), the Magpie (E4, page 36), the Bluebottle (C4, page 26) and the Black Swan (E5, page 37) all have arcs greater than 9¼˝. All blocks have an outer arc of 9¼˝, and any may be swapped into the center section. If you prefer to have a different block placed in the center section, the original square background needs to be trimmed. Swap the original inner arcs from these blocks with others if preferred.

1. Select the new blocks that will be used in the center section.

2. Place a Pattern Q arc on the back of the background fabric, aligning straight edges. Mark the outer curved section and trim fabric ¼˝ outside the newly marked curve.

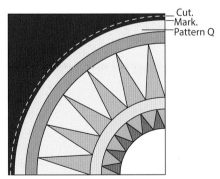

Mark and trim block.

3. Pin the extending arcs to the blocks at the quarter-points.

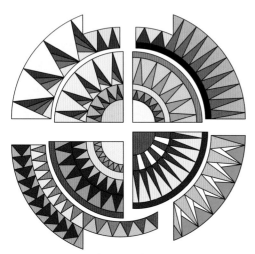

Attach extending arcs.

4. Hand baste first and then machine stitch in place.

5. Complete the blocks.

6. Add a Pattern P to any blocks that were removed from the center section.

JOINING THE CENTER BLOCKS

1. Join the extended blocks on the vertical seam up to the extended Cassowary Unit G arc.

2. Join the end of Cassowary Unit G to Black Swan Unit E.

3. Matching mid- and quarter-points, complete the Cassowary–Black Swan unit.

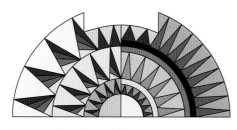

Sew vertical seams.

4. Matching the mid- and quarter-points of the Peacock and the Bluebottle–Magpie unit on the curved edge, hand baste and then machine stitch in place, stopping and starting your stitching ¼″ from the end of the seam.

5. Repeat with the Peacock Too and Cassowary–Black Swan unit.

6. Join the 2 sections together, matching seams where possible.

Insert Peacock and Peacock Too.

CORNER BLOCKS

1. Select the blocks for the corners of the center section.

2. Referring to the diagram below, use the required Pattern R or R(rev). Orientation is very important here. Pattern R is marked to assist correct orientation.

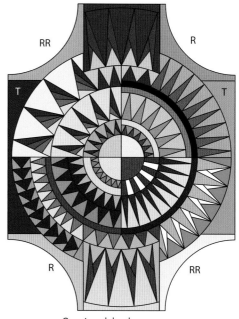

Setting block corners.

3. Prepare the corners by either trimming back the original background fabric, using Pattern R, Setting Corner, or adding a Pattern R fabric for those in R position.

4. Prepare the corners of the remaining corner blocks in a similar manner, using Pattern R(rev) or adding a Pattern R(rev) fabric for those in RR position.

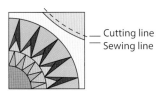 

— Cutting line
— Sewing line

Prepare corner blocks.

COMPLETING THE CENTER

1. Join a corner block to either end of Pattern T, 12″–15″ border fabric. Make 2 sets.

2. Matching quarter-points and seams, join the sets to the center unit.

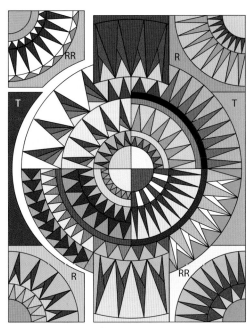

Complete center unit.

Assembly

The quilt is assembled in rows.

1. Using the photo of the quilt as placement guide, lay out the blocks in 8 rows of 7. Rearrange the blocks if needed until there is a pleasing mix of colors, ensuring that the alignment of the curves remains correct.

2. When placing the blocks, try to choose blocks that closely match at the 3″ circle and 9¼″ arc, as discrepancies at these points are more noticeable than mismatches at other points.

3. Matching seams, join the blocks for each unit and then press.

Unit A is 7 blocks across by 2 blocks high.

Unit B is 2 blocks across by 4 blocks high.

Unit C is 2 blocks across by 4 blocks high.

Unit D is 7 blocks across by 2 blocks high.

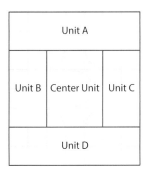

Join blocks for Units A–D.

JOINING THE UNITS

1. Sew Unit B to Center Unit to Unit C. Press.

2. Sew Unit A and Unit D to central panel. Press … and post a photo!

Border 1 is an optional ¼″-wide border used to separate the medium value blocks from the medium valued purple border. It may be omitted and Border 2 widened by an extra ¼″ if preferred. Fabric has been included in the directions for this to occur.

Borders 2, 3, and 4 form the main border. These are joined together before joining to the quilt.

Preparing the Border Templates

The border strip is pieced using freezer paper rather than regular foundation paper. If preferred, it may be pieced in the same manner as the blocks, in which case you can tape paper to form long strips and trace as per instructions.

Pattern U (short wedge border, pullout page P1), Pattern V (long wedge border, pullout page P1), and Pattern W (corner wedge border, pullout page P1) are provided. To draw Pattern UR (short wedge border reversed), Pattern VR (long wedge border reversed), and Pattern WR (corner wedge border reversed), place the original pattern facedown on a lightbox or bright window and trace.

SHORT BORDER

1. Cut a strip of freezer paper 13″ × 100″.

2. On the dull side of the freezer paper, use a mechanical pencil to trace 1 Pattern W (corner wedge border), 3 pairs of Pattern UR (short wedge border reversed) and Pattern U (short wedge border), and 1 Pattern WR (corner wedge border reversed) for the short borders, matching the outer edge and curves.

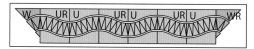

Short border

3. Erase the vertical lines between each pattern repeat. These wedges are not split.

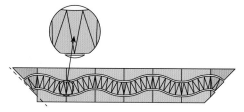

All wedges are full wedges.

4. Trim the lower edge of the border in line with the sloped edge of Patterns W and WR, using the 45° line on your ruler. Note that the sloped edges of the 3 patterns (inner, spiked, and outer) are *not* in a straight line at this stage.

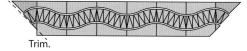

Trim corners.

5. Cut along the broken curved lines.

There are now 3 parts: the outer short border template, the spiked short border template, and the inner short border template. All parts have seam allowances on the curved sides. Label each part.

6. Place the outer border on top of the spiked border so the sewing lines are aligned and mark the matching points. Do the same with the inner border curve.

Mark matching points.

LONG BORDER

1. For the long border, cut a strip of freezer paper 13″ × 110″.

2. On the dull side of the freezer paper, use a mechanical pencil to trace 1 Pattern W, 4 pairs of Patterns VR and Pattern V, and 1 Pattern WR for the long borders, matching the outer edge and curves.

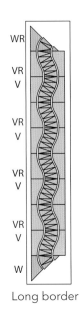

Long border

3. Trim the lower edge of the border in line with the inner curve of Patterns W and WR. Note that the sloped edges of the 3 patterns (inner, spiked, and outer) are *not* in a straight line at this stage.

4. Complete as per the short borders.

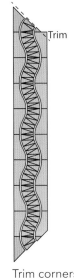

Trim corners.

PREPARING THE FABRIC TEMPLATES FOR THE SPIKED BORDERS

1. Cut 1 strip of freezer paper 6½″ × width.

2. On the dull side of the freezer paper, use a mechanical pencil to trace Pattern NW (narrow wedge, pullout page P3), Pattern WW (wide wedge, pullout page P3), and Pattern CW (corner wedge, pullout page P3). The seam allowance is included in the patterns.

3. Label and cut apart, using craft scissors.

Fabric

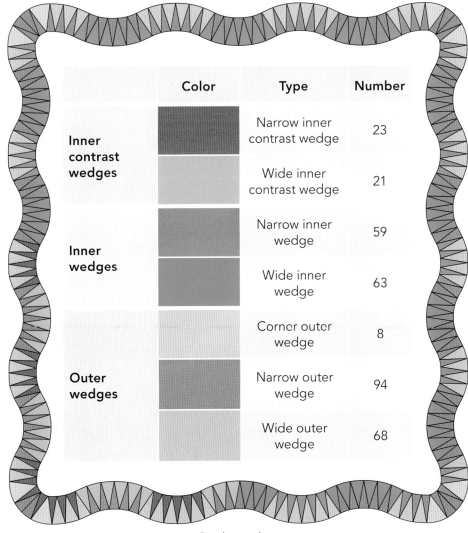

	Color	Type	Number
Inner contrast wedges		Narrow inner contrast wedge	23
		Wide inner contrast wedge	21
Inner wedges		Narrow inner wedge	59
		Wide inner wedge	63
Outer wedges		Corner outer wedge	8
		Narrow outer wedge	94
		Wide outer wedge	68

Border wedges

MATERIALS

Dark purple-black print: ⅓ yard for Border 1

Purple batik: 1⅔ yards for Border 2

Striped mustard: 20″ for Border 3 spikes

Mustard print: 2½ yards for Border 3 spikes and bias binding

Red fire print: 4 yards for Borders 3 and 4

CUTTING

WOF = width of fabric. LOF = length of fabric.
Starch all fabrics before cutting to minimize stretching.

Dark purple-black print

• Cut 8 strips 1½″ × WOF.

Purple batik

• Cut 6 strips 6″ × LOF.

Note: Fabric has been allowed for Border 1 to be omitted. If including Border 1, cut strips 5½″ wide or make as instructed and trim later as described in Adjusting Width of Border 1 (page 56).

Striped mustard

• Cut 3 strips 6½″ × WOF; using Pattern NW, subcut 9 wedges for short lower border and 14 wedges for long left border; using Pattern WW, subcut 9 wedges for short lower border and 12 wedges for long left border.

Mustard print

• Cut 1 strip 36″ × WOF; subcut 1 square 36″ × 36″ for bias binding.

• Cut 8 strips 6½″ × WOF; using Pattern NW, subcut 9 wedges for short lower border, 9 wedges for long left border, 18 wedges for short top border, and 23 wedges for long right border. Using Pattern WW, subcut 9 wedges for lower border, 12 wedges for long left border, 18 wedges for short upper border, and 24 wedges for long right border.

Red fire print

• Cut 4 strips 6½″ × WOF for wedges; using Pattern CW, subcut 8 wedges; using Pattern WW, subcut 50 wedges.

• Cut 2 strips 6″ × LOF for long borders.

• Cut 1 strip 6½″ × WOF for wedges; using Pattern WW, subcut 11 wedges.

• Cut 2 strips 6″ × LOF for short borders.

• Cut 14 strips 6½″ × WOF for wedges; using Pattern WW, subcut 7 wedges; using Pattern NW, subcut 94 wedges.

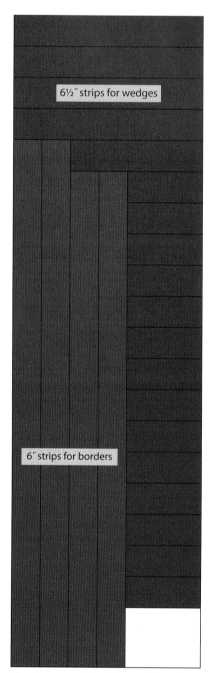

6½″ strips for wedges

6″ strips for borders

Cutting outer borders and wedges

Completing the Borders

BORDER 1

1. Join dark purple-black print strips end to end using 45° seams.

2. Press the seams open and cut 2 strips 1½″ × 72″ and 2 strips 1½″ × 82″.

3. Pin-mark 1″ in from the ends of all strips and at 10″ intervals; adjust this measurement if your blocks are not 10″ finished size.

BORDER 2

1. Join purple batik strips end to end, press, and cut 2 strips 6″ × 80″ and 2 strips 6″ × 90″.

2. Draw a line ¼″ from a long edge parallel to the side.

3. Matching the middles, and with *the curved edge to the marked line*, press the inner border freezer-paper template to the wrong side of the fabric strip. Trace around the template, extending the sloped line to the fabric edge. Mark the matching points. This is the sewing line.

Place template on fabric.

4. Do not cut at this stage.

BORDER 3

Piecing Border 3: Spiked Border

 Tip

Note that these are very long strips and may be awkward. If preferred, you may subcut into smaller units, cutting along one edge of a wedge. Add seam allowances to the new ends, piece each smaller unit, and join the units together.

Take care when rejoining that the straight edge remains in line.

The spiked borders were foundation pieced on freezer paper, but Vilene or foundation paper may be used if preferred. *If foundation piecing with freezer paper, remember to stitch beside the marked lines and not through the paper.* Complete all 4 borders, using your preferred method. When complete, stitch a stabilizing line each side a scant ¼″ out from the solid outer lines. Trim the curved sides carefully and remove the paper if used.

BORDER 4

1. Join red fire print strips end to end, press, and cut 2 strips 6″ × 80″ and 2 strips 6″ × 90″.

2. Draw a line ¼″ in parallel to a long edge.

3. Matching the middles, and with *the curved edge to the marked line*, press the outer border freezer-paper template to the wrong side of the fabric strip. Trace around the template, extending the sloped line to the fabric edge. This is the sewing line.

4. Do not cut at this stage.

Joining the Borders

Borders 2, 3, and 4 are joined before being attached to the quilt center.

1. Cut ¼″ from the curved edge of a short inner border. Only cut a small distance ahead of where you are sewing to minimize stretch.

Sewing line
Cutting line

Cut the border fabric.

2. Match the previously marked points of the inner border and the spiked border and pin to secure.

3. Hand baste in place and then machine stitch to secure.

4. Press the seam allowance away from the spiked border.

5. Repeat, sewing the outer border to the other side of the spiked border.

6. Repeat with all 4 borders.

Attaching the Borders

BORDER 1

Note: *This border has a finished width of only ¼˝. It was added as a value contrast as both the purple batik and many of the blocks were of medium value. It also allows adjustments to be made so the outer border will fit the joined blocks if needed.*

1. Matching the pins to the seams between the blocks stitch the long borders in place.

2. Press the seam allowance outward and trim to match the quilt edges.

3. Matching the pins to the seams between the blocks stitch the short borders in place.

4. Press the seam allowance outward and trim to match the quilt edges.

Adjusting Width of Border 1

1. Complete and join the border sections: Border 2, spiked Border 3, and Border 4.

2. This section was attached by hand to the quilt center due to the small size of Border 1. On the wrong side of the fabric, mark the sewing line for Border 2.

3. Measure the length of the inner seam of Border 2, excluding the seam allowance.

4. The outer side length of Border 1 *must* equal the inner side length of Border 2. By adjusting the width of Border 1, it is possible to fit these borders together perfectly.

5. Complete the following chart with measurements from your quilt to determine the finished width of Border 1.

6. On the back of the Border 1 fabric, draw a line to show the next *sewing line* so that the outer length of Border 1 equals the inner length of Border 2. Don't trim at this stage as it will be too awkward to work with.

From the above chart, Border 1 was only ¼˝ finished and so I drew my sewing line ¼˝ from the previous sewing line.

	The Wedding Quilt	Your quilt
Quilt center finished length	90˝	
Border 2 inner length	90½˝	
Difference between measurements	½˝	
Half of the difference = finished width of the border	¼˝	
Plus seam allowance (2˝ × ¼˝)	¾˝	
Quilt finished width (short side)	70˝	
Border 2 inner length (short side)	70½˝	
Difference between measurements	½˝	
Half of the difference = finished width of the border	¼˝	
Plus seam allowance	¾˝	

BORDERS 2, 3, AND 4

1. Stitch Border 2/3/4 strips to Border 1. *Do not* sew into the seam allowance at the corners.

2. Attach all 4 borders in the same manner.

3. Stitch the mitered seams to complete the border.

4. Press the seam allowance outward.

5. *Note:* *If Border 1 is omitted then Border 2 inner edge may need to be adjusted. Border 2 must match the finished length of the quilt center and is most likely to be too long. Measure your quilt and adjust where needed using the chart to help. Obtaining the correct length may also affect the height of Border 2.*

Join the borders.

Finishing

1. Cut 9 yards of backing fabric into 3 equal lengths.

2. Join together at the selvage, using ½˝ seams.

3. Cut the selvages off and press the seams to one side. Gently press the quilt top.

4. Lay the backing, right side down, on a large flat surface and tape or clip it down.

5. Layer the batting and quilt top (right side up) onto the backing, gently smoothing out each layer as you go.

6. Baste the 3 layers together in a 3˝-grid pattern.

Quilting

The Wedding Quilt was free-motion ditch-stitched throughout, in thread color to match the fabric. The plain background areas were free-motioned, either tracing designs in the fabric or extending the straight lines from the spikes. The purple batik and red borders were hand stitched with lines echoing the curves. The spikes were free-motion quilted with flames in the red and falling rain in the mustard. Use of walking foot to quilt the curves and spikes was not feasible due to the size of the quilt.

Quilting details

Binding

PREPARING THE QUILT FOR BINDING

As there are so many curves and bias edges, particularly in the border, extra care needs to be taken to ensure the quilt is flat.

1. Using 2 or more long rulers, draw a line on the right side of the quilt at the place you think will be the edge of your finished quilt. This line needs to be the same distance from the dark purple border on all sides.

2. Place a pin at the corner of the dark purple border. Measuring from that point to the edge of the quilt, draw a quarter-circle around the corner.

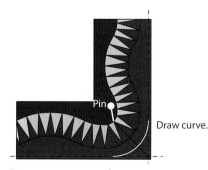

Draw curve.

Draw curve on each corner.

3. Using the longest stitch on your machine, stitch these lines in a thread color that is easily seen.

4. *Do not* trim extra fabric from the sides or corners until *after the binding has been sewn on.*

5. Measure the quilt length along the sides and through the middle.

6. If the measurements differ, average the lengths to find your target length.

● *Tip: Adjusting a Side Length*

1. Working on the back of your quilt and using a different thread color, sew 2 basting rows along the straight sections of the quilt edge, one just inside the seam allowance and another ½″ further in.

2. Leave a tail of thread at both ends of these stitching lines on each border. Tie the thread ends together on the back of the quilt.

3. On the top side of the quilt, pull the thread up slightly on one end and tie the ends together. Carefully pull up the loose threads to bring the quilt into the required size.

4. Gently spread the excess bulk throughout the entire side. The sides should now be the same length as the middle of the quilt.

CONTINUOUS BIAS BINDING

As the outer edge of *The Wedding Quilt* has curved corners, it is necessary to cut the binding on the bias. Binding cut along the straight grain of the fabric will neither sit flat nor bend around the curves. The following method generates a long continuous

strip of bias binding. Take care when pressing and sewing to not stretch the fabric. Starch the fabric before beginning.

1. Label 2 opposite sides of the 36″ fabric square (see Cutting, Red Fire Print, page 54) as A and B, and cut diagonally.

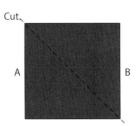

Label and cut.

2. Using a slightly shorter stitch length, with right sides facing, offset the ends ¼″, match the labeled sides, and sew the triangles together. Press the seams open.

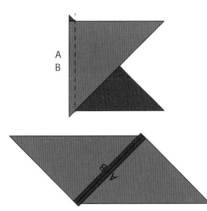

Stitch and press seam open.

3. On the reverse of the fabric, mark a line ¼″ from the top edge. Mark parallel lines across the fabric at 2″ intervals. Label the lines as shown.

Draw and label lines.

4. Fold the fabric, right sides together, aligning the raw numbered edges and carefully matching the numbers (1 to 1, 2 to 2, and so on). Pin to secure forming a tube. **Note:** *Neither 0 (zero) nor the highest number is matched.*

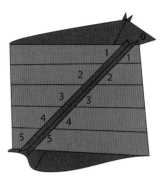

Match numbers, pin, and stitch.

5. Using a ¼″ seam and a slightly shorter stitch length, machine stitch the pinned seam. Press the seam open. It is necessary to rotate the tube to press the seam.

6. Using fabric scissors, cut along the marked line, spiraling around the tube. If using a rotary cutter, place the cutting mat inside the formed tube and be careful to only cut one layer at a time.

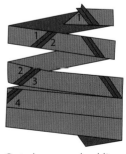

Cut along marked line.

7. Taking great care not to stretch the strip, press the binding in half lengthwise with the wrong sides together.

ATTACHING THE BINDING

1. Pin the binding into place around the quilt, matching the raw edges of the binding with the first sewn line of basted stitches on the border.

2. Using a walking foot, a ¼″ seam with thread color to match your binding, and starting about 8″ from the end of the strip and halfway along one side, stitch the binding to the front of the quilt through all layers. Be careful not to stretch the binding. There is no need to stop stitching ¼″ from the corner; simply continue stitching carefully and work around the corner.

3. Sew around all sides of the quilt; stop stitching about 8″ from the starting point and remove the quilt from the machine.

4. Make a 45° fold at the end of the starting strip and press.

5. Lay the folded strip end onto the other end and mark the fold on the other end.

Mark fold.

6. Move the binding strips away from the quilt and match the fold line with the drawn line and sew together.

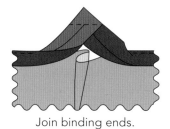

Join binding ends.

7. Trim the seam allowances to ¼″, press open, and refold binding.

8. Finish sewing binding to the quilt top.

9. Remove the extra basting lines.

10. Trim ¼″ *beyond* the raw edges of the binding to allow for a fuller binding.

11. Fold the binding to the wrong side of the quilt and then slip-stitch in place.

12. Label the quilt with your name and date.

Quilt label

Gallery

Dreamtime at the Waterhole, 56½″ × 67¾″,
designed by Cinzia White, made by Jannette Jackson, 2019

Blue Whale blocks (page 33)

Southern Lights, 28″ × 28″,
designed by Cinzia White, made by Marilyn Kellett, 2019

Fairy Penguin blocks (page 24)

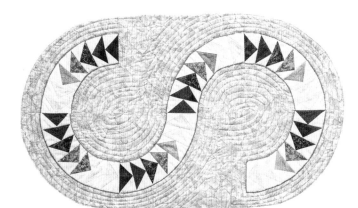

Swirling Birds, 19″ × 32″,
designed by Cinzia White, made by Joy L. Cook, 2019

Blue Whale blocks (page 33)

Nebulae, 20½″ × 20½″,
designed by Cinzia White, made by Val Nielsen, 2019

Fairy Penguin blocks (page 24)

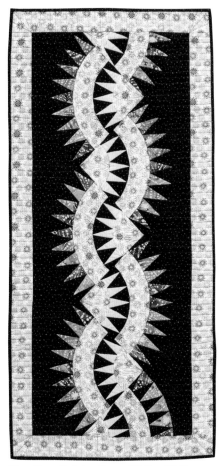

New Year Celebrations, 19½″ × 42¼″,
designed by Cinzia White,
made by Sandra Pearce, 2019

Bandicoot blocks (page 41)

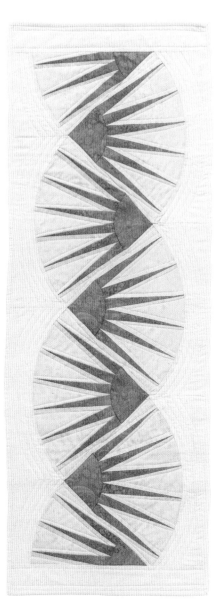

Waves Upon the Sand, 16″ × 43″,
designed by Cinzia White,
made by Marilyn Pepper, 2019

Fairy Penguin blocks (page 24)

Complicated Fun, 20½″ × 60″,
designed by Cinzia White,
made by Maggie Froggatt, 2019

Bottlenose blocks (page 39)
are scaled at 70%.

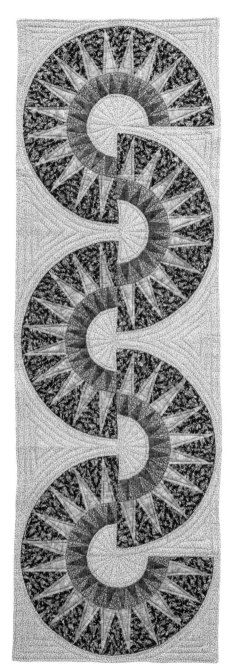

Strolling Through the Garden, 19″ × 57½″,
designed by Cinzia White,
made by Eunice Creed, 2019

Bottlenose blocks (page 39)

Mum's Gift, 28″ × 83″,
designed by Cinzia White,
made by Helen Hawes, 2019

Brolga blocks (page 17)

Drought and Fire, 23½″ × 46½″,
designed by Cinzia White,
made by Marilyn Hinwood, 2019

Bluebottle blocks (page 26)
are scaled at 80%.

About the Author

CINZIA WHITE has been quilting for more than 30 years. This is her second sampler book following on from her hexagon sampler, *The Storyteller's Sampler Quilt* (from C&T Publishing). She has also published numerous patterns in most Australian and some American patchwork magazines and has taught throughout Australia.

Influenced by her mathematics teaching background, Cinzia enjoys designing traditional quilts that are based on geometric designs. With perseverance and a desire to explore new directions, she has created many award-winning quilts.

Cinzia loves working with color and often with no prearranged plan. She has a tendency to incorporate points and curves into her intricate patterns that alternate between two distinct styles: one scrappy and haphazard, the other involving intricate handwork.

It was through a need to finish a quilt quickly, for her son PJ and Khanam's wedding, that *The Wedding Quilt* was made. The accuracy and speed of foundation piecing New York Beauty blocks were perfect for this project.

Visit Cinzia online and follow on social media!

WEBSITE: cinziawhite.com

FACEBOOK: /mycinziawhitedesigns

Also check out Cinzia's Facebook group "Dazzling New York Beauty Sampler" for more inspiration and sharing!

Photo by Aimee Kirkham, Oxford Photography

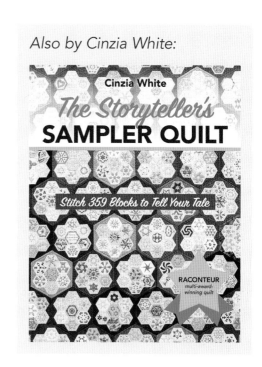

Also by Cinzia White: